∞

A Pocket Retreat
for Catholics

F. Maucourant

A Pocket Retreat for Catholics

Thirty Steps to Holiness —
in Just Ten Minutes a Day!

SOPHIA INSTITUTE PRESS®
Manchester, New Hampshire

A *Pocket Retreat for Catholics* was formerly published in 1911 in New York, Cincinnati, and Chicago by Benziger Brothers, under the title *The Life of Union with Our Divine Lord*. In this 2000 edition by Sophia Institute Press® some quotations from each chapter have been omitted and minor editorial revisions to the 1911 edition have been made.

Sophia Institute Press®
Box 5284, Manchester, NH 03108
1-800-888-9344
www.sophiainstitute.com

Nihil obstat: Henry S. Bowden, *Censor Deputatus*
Imprimatur: Edm. Can. Surmont, *Vicarius Generalis*
Westmonasterii, February 23, 1911

Library of Congress Cataloging-in-Publication Data

Maucourant, F.
    [Life of union with our Divine Lord]
    A pocket retreat for Catholics : thirty steps to holiness
in just ten minutes a day / F. Maucourant.
        p. cm.
    Previously published: A life of union with our Divine
Lord. New York : Benziger Brothers, 1911.
    Includes bibliographical references.
    ISBN: 1-928832-12-1 (pbk. : alk. paper)
    1. Spiritual life — Catholic Church. 2. Meditations.
I. Title.

BX2350.2.M372 2000
248.4′82 — dc21   00-038789

02 03 04 05 10 9 8 7 6 5 4 3

∞

Contents

Editor's Notes

The biblical quotations in the following pages are based on the Douay-Rheims edition of the Old and New Testaments. Where applicable, quotations have been cross-referenced with the differing names and enumeration in the Revised Standard Version, using the following symbol: (RSV =).

The original edition of this work sometimes provided less than adequate documentation of the sources quoted. In those cases, we endeavored to discover complete information, and, where that was not possible, we have provided as much information about the source as we were able to find.

∞

Preface

It is the chief aim of these meditations to lead simple
and generous souls to a still greater and more generous
love of God, and to a closer union with Him who already
loves them with a tender love. As our Redeemer, He has
already raised us from the rank of servants to be "fellow
citizens with the saints" and "friends" of the Savior.[1]

Many live in a state of fear or timid reverence that
hinders them from drawing nearer to the Heart of their
divine Master. Such persons must learn that the short ·
est and quickest way to go to Him is the way of love,
a constant and tender love that leads them to imitate
Him. They must live as Jesus lived, in the innermost
depths of their souls, and manifest this inner life in
every detail of their daily actions. Nothing can give

[1]   Eph. 2:19; John 15:14.

them more encouragement in this than the words of the Holy Gospel: "Tell ye the daughter of Sion, 'Behold, thy King cometh unto thee, meek' ";[2] and the words of our Lord Himself: "Abide in my love"[3] — i.e., in union with me.

"His infinite majesty deserves our deepest respect and veneration," says St. Alphonsus,[4] "but He prefers to be treated with loving confidence, rather than with obedience dictated by fear, on the part of those souls who love Him."

"Interior peace, spiritual joy, light, consolation, and strength are the real fruits, the sure recompense, of this union with our Lord and with His divine Heart, burning with love for us. These fruits will abound more and more, in proportion as our communion with Him becomes more frequent, more tender, and closer still. Our Lord Jesus takes pleasure in thus preparing His faithful friends for the perfect happiness reserved for them in Heaven by this sweet foretaste of heavenly consolation. How

[2] Matt. 21:5.

[3] John 15:9.

[4] St. Alphonsus Liguori (1696-1767), founder of the Redemptorists.

terribly deluded, then, are those timid souls who fear to approach our Lord, or to speak to Him, heart to heart, as one friend speaks to another! Of how many graces and spiritual favors are not they deprived by thus distrusting their good Master!"[5]

Such teaching as this seems well calculated to encourage and dilate our souls, to impress us with the truth that God is a kind Master, to strengthen our resolution to accept His love, and to lead us to follow our Savior in the way of sacrifice and perfection; for it is far easier to adore a God who is tender and full of loving-kindness. The joy inspired by such convictions will encourage us to give our Lord that proof of true love which consists in leading a holy life. And thus will be realized the desire of St. Ignatius,[6] the holy author of the *Spiritual Exercises:* "I will ask for an intimate knowledge of our Lord, who became man for me, in order that I may love Him more fervently and follow Him more closely."

[5] R. P. Servière, S.J.
[6] St. Ignatius Loyola (c. 1491-1556), founder of the Jesuits.

Come, Holy Spirit

Come, Holy Spirit, Creator, come
from Thy bright heavenly throne!
Come, take possession of our souls,
and make them all Thine own!
Thou who art called the Paraclete,
best gift of God above,
the living spring, the living fire,
sweet unction, and true love!
Thou who are sevenfold in Thy grace,
finger of God's right hand,
His promise, teaching little ones
to speak and understand!
Oh, guide our minds with Thy blest light,
with love our hearts inflame,
and with Thy strength, which ne'er decays,
confirm our mortal frame.
Far from us drive our hellish foe,
true peace unto us bring,
and through all perils guide us safe
beneath Thy sacred wing.
Through Thee may we the Father know,
Through Thee, the eternal Son,
and Thee, the Spirit of Them both,
thrice-blessed Three in One.
All glory to the Father be,
and to the risen Son;
the same to Thee, O Paraclete,
while endless ages run. Amen.

∽

How to make this retreat

On the day you begin these exercises, recite the "Come, Holy Spirit,"[7] and entrust their success to the Sacred Heart of Jesus. Then place yourself under the protection of those saints who have been special friends of our dear Lord, and invoke them often during the month: the Blessed Virgin, under her title of Our Lady of Good Counsel, St. Joseph, St. John, St. Mary Magdalene, St. Francis of Assisi, St. Anthony of Padua, St. Teresa, St. Gertrude, St. Mechtildis, St. Rose of Lima, and St. Margaret Mary Alacoque.[8]

[7] See opposite page.

[8] St. Francis of Assisi (c. 1182-1225), founder of the Franciscan Order; St. Anthony of Padua (1195-1231), Franciscan friar; probably St. Teresa of Avila (1515-1582), Carmelite nun and mystic; probably St. Gertrude the Great (1256-c. 1302), German mystic; St.

After each meditation, make a very precise resolution, and not only observe it during the day, but be determined to make it the practice of your whole life. Take note of it in writing, so that you may refer to it at the end of the month and see what progress you have made in the spiritual life.

Make your special examination of conscience every day, so that it may help you to practice what you have learned during your meditation.

Ask our Lord, by frequent aspirations — that is, brief, spontaneous prayers — the grace to understand His loving call and to respond to it simply and courageously.

Mechtildis of Helfta (c. 1241-1298), novice-mistress of St. Gertrude the Great; St. Rose of Lima (1586-1617), Third Order Dominican and first canonized saint of the Americas; St. Margaret Mary Alacoque (1647-1690), Visitation nun and chief founder of devotion to the Sacred Heart of Jesus. — ED.

∽

A Pocket Retreat
for Catholics

Step One

∞

Answer Christ's invitation
to a life of union with Him

Jesus is the "divine Beloved," the "all fair." Everything that is done by this heavenly "Beggar for our love" leads to those words which express His tender desires: "As the Father hath loved me, I also have loved you. Abide in my love,"[9] i.e., in union with me. To such an extent, to such excess, His goodness reaches out to us.

Now, let us consider, first, what is this life of union with Jesus and, second, what souls are called to it.

∞

Union involves thought, feeling, and action

Union means perfect similarity of thought, feeling, and action with the beloved one, so that, in the end,

[9] John 15:9.

3

the two become one. Now, this life of union with Jesus is not only a possibility for us; it is our real vocation ever since He deigned to say, "Abide in my love."

Union in thought. Our thoughts must be good if we think as God thinks. God is infinite and uncreated Wisdom; our own minds are a "light from the countenance of God, signed upon us,"[10] and Jesus Himself is called by St. John "the true Light, which enlighteneth every man that cometh into this world."[11]

What divine light shone in Adam's soul before the thick shadows were thrown over it by Original Sin! What splendors shone in the holy soul of Jesus, the second Adam, made in the image of God! What radiance beams from the face of a saint, one of those pure souls whose privilege it is to penetrate deeply, even in this life, into the secrets of God!

If I make these meditations earnestly and generously, they will teach me how to direct my thoughts by giving me new ideas of God, and of Jesus, that sweetest thought in the mind of God. Above all things, I will ask for an intimate knowledge of that Lord, who became man for

[10] Cf. Ps. 4:7 (RSV = Ps. 4:6).
[11] John 1:9.

me, so that I may love Him more tenderly and follow Him more closely.

Union in feeling. The apostle St. Paul said, "Let this mind be in you, which was also in Christ Jesus."[12] Our Savior took possession of and purified our hearts so that they might become as His Heart, when He prayed to His Father thus: "That the love wherewith Thou hast loved me may be in them, and I in them."[13] This is why He calls us His "friends,"[14] the familiar friends of God, "fellow citizens with the saints and the domestics of God."[15]

Jesus also calls Himself the spouse of our souls: "I will espouse thee to me forever, as a bridegroom decked with a crown";[16] and God seems to dwell upon this comparison not as we, with our limited ideas, might imagine, but by investing it with every possible conception of sweetness and union. True piety consists in thinking of God and the individual soul as two devoted, loving, and trusting friends for all eternity. Such a thought will teach us

[12] Phil. 2:5.
[13] John 17:26.
[14] John 15:15.
[15] Eph. 2:19.
[16] Osee 2:19 (RSV = Hos. 2:19); Isa. 61:10.

to love Him with wisdom and will fill us with tender joy. But after all, whenever we speak or think of God, may we not say that there is something beyond, higher and deeper still, which we can never penetrate?

Union in action. Jesus is our model. Our love, like His, must consist of works rather than words. Like Him, at all hours and in whatever work we may be engaged, we must try to say, "I must be about my Father's business."[17] Then we shall be entirely occupied with divine things — Jesus Himself acting through us and God acting with us, until, as St. Francis de Sales[18] says, we have "Jesus in our head, our heart, our hands, our tongue, our eyes, our ears, and our feet."

Nevertheless, there are some actions of our Savior beyond our powers, such as curing the sick, raising the dead, and other miracles. But can we forget the promise of our Master: "He that believeth in me, the works that I do shall he do also; and greater works than these shall he do, because I go to the Father"?[19] If there are few miracles now, it is because there are few souls who give

[17] Luke 2:49.

[18] St. Francis de Sales (1567-1622), Bishop of Geneva.

[19] John 14:12.

their consent to be the instruments of such things and do the work of God. Our lives are barren, because we are governed by self-love. And when we can understand that God desires to work with us in all our actions, we shall act as the saints have acted.

∞

Christ calls you to a life of union with Him

Is a life of union with Jesus a special vocation — for priests, religious, saints, privileged persons, and mystical souls? Not at all.

This trusting and tender union with God is the very foundation of Christianity. There is no exception made to that call of our Savior: "Come unto me"; and for those who might imagine that the labors, cares, and sorrows of this life might hold them back, He adds, "Come unto me, all you that labor and are heavy-laden, and I will refresh you."[20]

There are hours when we are all mystics; we throw ourselves instinctively upon the Sacred Heart of Jesus whenever sorrow or pain strikes us or when we feel the need of carrying our joys to a safe refuge.

[20] Matt. 11:28.

God does not ask of us the mysticism of hermits, and there have been saints in every state of life, in every vocation, and in every society.

St. Francis de Sales says, "Devotion ought to be practiced differently by a prince and by a workman; by a widow, a virgin, and a married woman. It must be regulated by bodily strength and the affairs and duties of each one. But in whatever state of life we may be, we all can and ought to aspire to the life of perfection."

St. Catherine of Siena charmed the Heart of her heavenly Spouse by her patience, her elevations of soul, and her ecstasies of contemplation; but I take quite as much pleasure in looking upon her in her father's kitchen, stirring the fire, cooking the meat, kneading the bread, and doing all the servile work of the house. Her father was, for her, our Lord; her mother our Lady; and her brothers the Apostles. Every one of her actions was an offering of service to the Divine Majesty and the court of Heaven.

Therefore, there is no real obstacle to this life of union with God — either age, or station of life, or health, or any duty whatever. The perfect life consists in living the life of Jesus, as far as is possible to human infirmity. Also, it is in this sense that our Lord says to

His chosen ones, "Come, follow me."[21] And at His call, they leave all: father, mother, brother, sisters, and the world, to choose "the better part";[22] they renounce all other friendships to consecrate their souls, their hearts, and their whole being to Jesus.

∞

Affections

Grant to me, O Father
most holy and most merciful,
wisdom to understand Thy intentions with
regard to me, a heart to share Thy feelings,
courage to seek Thee alone, and a way
of life that contributes to Thy glory.

Give me, O my God,
eyes that may see only Thee,
a tongue that may speak only of Thee,
and a life devoted entirely to Thy will.

Finally, O my Savior, grant me the joy
of seeing Thee one day, face-to-face,
with all Thy saints in glory.

St. Benedict

---

[21] Mark 10:21.
[22] Luke 10:42.

∽

Examination of Conscience
* *Did I begin these meditations in a right spirit, determined to seek light?*

* *If I found them too exalted, or too perfect for me, was it because of cowardice, fear of undertaking too much, or carelessness?*

* *In my thoughts, preferences, feelings, and conversation, is there anything not in conformity with the maxims of the Gospel, anything that Jesus condemns or which He could not bless?*

* *Have I asked for grace to find in these meditations a means of living more closely in the friendship of my dear Savior?*

∽

Resolution
Here, and at the same point in each step hereafter, make a resolution to practice what you learned from this meditation.

∽

Spiritual Bouquet
"Abide in my love. . . . I have called you friends."

John 15:9, 15

Step Two

∞

Recognize the love with which God created you

"To obtain a true love of God," says St. Ignatius, "I will recall to my memory all the benefits I have received from Him: those which are common to all, such as creation and Redemption; and those which are special to myself, individually, considering very affectionately all that God, our Lord, has done for me, all that He has given me, and how much He desires to give me Himself."

In contemplating God as our Creator, beholding Him acting and providing for us by means of created objects, we begin to learn that science of true love which consists of works rather than words.

First, let us consider the fact that God created man through love, and then let us consider our first union with God.

∞

God longs to bestow His gifts on you
"The Lord hath made all things for Himself."[23]
"Imperfect creatures, such as we are," says St. Thomas,[24]
"are obliged to labor for all we possess, to satisfy our
wants and necessities, and our self-love; but God, who
is perfect, has no other end in view but to manifest His
perfections." "If thou art without God," says St. Augustine,[25] "thou art indeed poor; and if thou art with God,
He is none the richer." God is sufficient for Himself;
nothing can add to His perfection or His happiness.

It follows, then, that God has need of no one.

"But there are two ways," says St. Thomas, "of
needing someone: the necessity of the poor man, who
stretches out his hand to receive, and the necessity of
the rich man, who opens his heart to give." God is love;
God is goodness. His first act is to be Himself; His second act is to give Himself to men. The natural inclination of God — if we may so speak, His temperament,

---

[23] Prov. 16:4.

[24] St. Thomas Aquinas (c. 1225-1274), Dominican phi-
losopher, theologian, and Doctor of the Church.

[25] St. Augustine (354-430), Bishop of Hippo.

His character — is to be good to His creatures and to give Himself to them. To such an extent is this true that St. Teresa says, "If all created souls were to forsake Him, they would deprive Him of one of His joys."

"He does not desire a happy solitude, nor a lonely beatitude," says St. Gregory Nazianzen,[26] and not being able to give away all that He is, He gives all that He has. This infinite love, this river of infinite felicity, which flows from the Father to the Son, and from the Son to the Holy Spirit, He allowed one day to invade humanity and raise it to a state of beatitude.

St. Francis de Sales clearly explains these mysterious relations: "Man has a great need and a great capacity for receiving benefits, and God has great abundance and a great inclination to bestow them. And we can scarcely say which has the greater pleasure — Infinite Goodness in bestowing favors, or extreme poverty in receiving them. The Divine Mercy takes more pleasure in bestowing His graces than we feel in receiving them."

Our Lord Himself said to St. Mechtildis, "I am a torrent which desires to overflow. I wish to make vessels

[26] St. Gregory Nazianzen (329-389), Bishop of Constantinople and Father and Doctor of the Church.

for myself, that I may fill them with the waters of my love." Love is that "sweet tyrant" which has drawn God out of Himself and made Him seek His own glory, not for Himself, but for us. St. Irenaeus[27] says, "God did not create man because He had any need of him, but He felt the need of some being upon whom to bestow His gifts."

But what of Christ, our blessed Lord — what share had He in our happiness, in the hour of creation? All things were made by Him — the Eternal Wisdom, whose "delight is to be with the children of men."[28] His work is accomplished when He draws from nothingness those souls who are to live with Him as friends. And at last, one day, He will even say to one of His creatures these wonderful words: "I could not be entirely happy if it were not for thee."[29]

∽

God gives Himself to you in many ways
"The root of all things," says St. Thomas, "is mercy"; and creation is the first almsgiving that Infinite Love

[27] St. Irenaeus (c. 130-c. 200), Bishop of Lyons.
[28] Prov. 8:31.
[29] *Revelations of St. Gertrude*.

has bestowed upon utter misery and destitution. "I have loved thee with an everlasting love; therefore, have I drawn thee."[30]

But why were we created? And why does God love us so much?

It is St. Augustine who gives us the answer, when he exclaims, "Thou hast made us for Thyself, O my God, and our heart findeth no rest until it reposeth in Thee."[31] To have God as our own God — to possess Him entirely — is the end of our creation.

God has many ways of giving Himself to us, even in this life. Creatures are "so many copies and reproductions of the Divine Perfection," St. Thomas tells us. They are the letters of His blessed Name, the fragrant marks of His footsteps, the echo of His words, and the reflected rays of His adorable face. "Heaven and earth, and all that they contain, cry out to me that I must love Thee, O my God," declared St. Augustine.

But as long as we are in this world, our knowledge and love of God are enveloped in darkness and resisted by a thousand imperfections on our part. What we need

[30] Jer. 31:3.
[31] *Confessions*, Bk. 1, ch. 1.

is such a knowledge of Him as will elevate our minds and give rest to our hearts.

Here shines forth the infinite goodness of God. After having given everything to His creature — to man, born a servant — He calls him His son and gives Himself: "I am thy protector and thy reward."[32] He gives us supernatural powers. He creates within us the capacity for heroic virtue. The distance that separates Him from us is filled up and bridged over. "We see now through glass in a dark manner; but then face-to-face."[33] "We know that when He shall appear, we shall be like Him, because we shall see Him as He is."[34]

How much He loved the first created man, when this wonderful union of God and man began, and how tenderly God taught His creature that "love consists in the mutual communication of gifts bestowed," as St. Ignatius says. Under the gently swinging shadows of the garden of delights, when the shades of evening fell, God took pleasure in visiting Adam, looking upon him, and speaking to him; and His divine presence, His look and

[32] Gen. 15:1.
[33] 1 Cor. 13:12.
[34] 1 John 3:2.

words, caused the heart of Adam to melt with love.
God made Adam the king of His dominions and filled
the heart of His creature with the fullness of His gifts.
He took delight in giving, as Adam did in receiving.

Now, the Holy Spirit has said of us, "I will draw
them with the cords of Adam, with the bands of
love."[35] Sin has broken these bands of love, but the
heart of God can never change, and whenever man
yields to His divine tenderness and consents to love his
Creator, he will find that merciful Father ready to give
Himself freely, to return love for love, and to forget the
past.

Every one of us must have known one of those precious hours when our good Master gives Himself to us,
perhaps after long absence — when we find ourselves
in Paradise, even upon earth. The gates of our Eden
may be closed sometimes, but the angel who holds the
drawn sword[36] is always ready to sheathe it and to open
to us, if the tears of our heart flow from our eyes, united
with the tears of our Redeemer, and are shed by us as a
token of great repentance and love.

[35] Osee 11:4 (RSV = Hos. 11:4).
[36] Cf. Gen. 3:24.

17

A Pocket Retreat for Catholics

∞
Affections

*My God, Thou who art sufficient in Thyself to all eternity,
Thou hast deigned through the extreme delicacy of Thine affection,
to have need of us, and now that Thou hast asked for our hearts,
with such infinite tenderness, shall we have the terrible courage
to refuse them to Thee? Thou dost ask for them, that Thou
mayest sanctify and bless them, and pour into them Thy gifts,
Thy love, and Thy divine beatitude! O God all-loving and
all-lovable, may our hearts belong to Thee alone!*

∞
Examination of Conscience

* *Have I often thought of thanking God for giving me life?*

* *Am I grateful to God for all His benefits?*

* *Do I make use of myself and of creatures, with
the respect due to everything that belongs to God,
of which I shall have to give an account?*

* *Do I try to give my good God the joy that
He desired to receive when He created me?*

* *Do I realize that any infidelity or act of indifference
on my part is to defeat the plans of God?*

* *What is it that really prevents me from being
very simple and familiar with my good God?*

∞
Resolution

∞
Spiritual Bouquet
"I am the Lord thy God. I am thy Love.
I created thee out of pure love,
that I might take my delight in thee."

Our Lord to St. Gertrude

Step Three

∽

Recognize your value in God's sight

St. Mechtildis saw the Angel of Mercy in Heaven interceding for sinful man. Clothed in a white garment, he approached God every day, presenting to Him the sins of men, until he obtained the promise of a Redeemer to come. After the Fall of man, love could no longer display itself; it had become justice, and the designs of God were frustrated. But the Supreme Master of the world was still a Father and could not endure the sight of the unhappy sinner. Then the coming of a Savior was promised, and at last He came.

Let us meditate on this; let us excite in ourselves "a lively desire to know more of the Incarnate Word of God, so that we may follow Him more nearly, serve Him more freely, and love Him more dearly." Let us contemplate, first, our Savior seeking after man and, second, man finding his Savior.

∽

God seeks you

"God so loved the world, as to give His only-begotten Son."[37]

When sin entered the world, fear reigned over the heart of man. He who had formerly been the friend and companion of God now dreaded the very sight of his Creator. He ran from God; he hid himself, for he had lost that innocence and holiness that had made him pleasing in God's sight.

What, then, can this good God do? The angels indeed are faithful to Him, but that was not the ideal of His dream; that was not the plan of His creation. Therefore, He will Himself go in pursuit of this poor, humbled, miserable humanity.

We can never understand why we have such value in the sight of God. We fail to see how He can take any pleasure in us, for we are not noble, as the man of His first creation; we are only remnants of humanity, failures, ruins — just as when we behold countenances aged and ravaged by time, we cannot understand the charm they exercised in their youth.

[37] John 3:16.

God wished to restore, by means of His Son, all that He had first given to man; and this time He gave Himself utterly. When we contemplate all the love bestowed upon us, "we might almost say that man has become the God of God Himself," says St. Augustine.

St. John of the Cross[38] has a sweet allegory about the Incarnation. He says, "The Father gave creation as a bride to His Son; but this bride became a slave, loaded with iron chains. The Father said to the Word, 'My Son, here is Thy bride, whom I made in Thine image, whom Thou didst love so much. To redeem her from slavery, Thou also must become like her, for such is the law of love. Take flesh like hers; she will be happier to see Thee so.' 'My will is Thine,' said the Eternal Word. 'I will go and find my bride; I will take upon my shoulders her sufferings and weariness; I will die, so that she may live, and so I will lead her back to my Father.' "

Therefore, the Incarnation was decided. "Drop down dew, ye heavens, from above, and let the clouds rain the just: let the earth be opened, and bud forth a Savior."[39]

---

[38] St. John of the Cross (1542-1591), mystical Doctor and joint founder of the Discalced Carmelites.

[39] Isa. 45:8.

"The Word was made flesh and dwelt among us."[40]
"For us men and for our salvation, He came down from Heaven."[41]

"Suffering humanity has nothing more to do now but to repose trustingly upon Christ," says St. Augustine, "and the Word, at His Resurrection, will carry His creature to Heaven." God condescended to stoop to man; and so He takes back the whole of creation to His embrace. He has placed man between the world of bodies and the world of spirits, as a bond of friendship and a pledge of affection. This order of things was destroyed by sin, but Christ has wonderfully restored it; henceforth, it is He who is the bond of friendship for every creature, the center of all worlds, the blessed Home where God gives the kiss of peace to all creation. "O my Christ," said St. Francis of Assisi, "Thou canst no longer defend Thyself against the madness of loving, for it was Love that drew Thee down to earth."

"God was made man, that man might become as God, as Christ became man," says St. Gregory Nazianzen. To what closer union could we aspire?

[40] John 1:14.
[41] Nicene Creed.

∞

Jesus shows you God's face

Ever since the promise of a Savior was given, humanity cried out to God, "O Lord, hear! O Lord, be appeased! . . . Delay not, for Thine own sake!"[42] The human race longed for God, and the Incarnation was, on God's part, an admirable way of satisfying that desire. "He that seeth me," said Jesus to St. Philip, "seeth the Father also."[43]

Origen[44] clearly explains this divine condescension. "Suppose," says he, "that a beautiful statue had been made — as large as the whole world. It would be quite impossible for us to contemplate it, on account of its immense size. Therefore, so that everyone might be able to see it, a small model was prepared. It was thus that the Divine Word humbled Himself, made Himself small and insignificant, presenting to us an admirable copy of His Father, so that now we may all dare to contemplate this lesser grandeur of the Divinity." Mary clothed the

[42] Dan. 9:19.

[43] John 14:9.

[44] Origen (c. 185-c. 254), Alexandrian biblical critic, exegete, theologian, and spiritual writer.

Divine Word with a garment of flesh, and since then, we can easily find God.

Thus "the goodness and kindness of God our Savior appeared."[45] Let us contemplate this infant Jesus — "made like unto us,"[46] a little child. St. Bernard[47] tells us, "As God, His greatness is above all other greatness, and commands our adoration; at Bethlehem, He is so small that He demands our love." A Virgin Mother has just given Him to the world; she holds Him in her arms and smiles in His sweet face. An aged man is allowed to carry Him and caress Him. Poor shepherds approach Him fearlessly and kiss His little feet and hands. He is the Lamb of God, He may say of Himself that His life is the life of sweetness itself. He desires also that His disciples shall be like lambs and learn of Him to be "meek and humble of heart."[48] He is indeed the good God, whom humanity has sought for so long.

Jesus, Savior, the whole world knows, the whole world says, how much Thou hast loved us! Thou hast loved the

---

[45] Titus 3:4.
[46] Cf. Heb. 2:17.
[47] St. Bernard (1090-1153), Abbot of Clairvaux.
[48] Matt. 11:29.

poor, for Thou didst choose poverty as Thy portion. Thou hast loved sinners — the despised publican, the sinful woman of Samaria, Magdalene, the woman who had "sinned much."[49] *Thou didst seek their company, so that Thy love might soften their hearts. It was for these beloved sinners that Thou didst speak those touching parables, so reassuring to the faint-hearted: those of the prodigal son, the Good Shepherd, and the lost sheep.*[50] *Thou didst love Thine enemies.*

Thou knowest me, and lovest me, now, just as if I had had the joy of living near Thee during Thy life on earth. Thou hast loved as no one else has ever loved, or ever will love. As Thy beloved disciple said, "God is love."[51]

This gentle Messiah came on earth as "the interpreter of the Divinity," St. Ambrose tells us.[52] Before His coming, men knew the infinite power of God, His profound wisdom, and the severity of His justice; but they knew nothing as yet of the excess of His mercy. In

[49] Cf. Luke 18:10-14; John 4:7 ff.; Mark 16:9; Luke 7:36-47.

[50] Cf. Luke 15:11-32; John 10:11-16; Luke 15:4-6.

[51] Cf. 1 John 4:8.

[52] St. Ambrose (c. 339-397), Bishop of Milan.

the person of the Savior, justice and peace embraced each other; and man, who had feared hitherto, began to love his Creator.

Christ was loved while on earth, and He is loved now, as no other man has been loved. He is the joy of our hearts. The little child begins to love Jesus, even in his mother's arms. Young men and maidens, when the storms of temptation attack them, seek refuge in the Heart of Jesus. They tell Him of their struggles and failures and implore the pardon that purifies, the counsel that guides, and the strength that supports. The man of ripe age finds rest at His feet, and the old man, drawing near his end and looking back on this world of disappointment and sorrow, says to the one Friend who has never deceived him, "To Thee I come."

The true secret of the zeal of all apostles, the heroism of all martyrs, the constancy of all confessors, and the purity of all virgins, is summed up in those words of St. Cecilia:[53] "I love my Christ." He desires to be the Protector, the Physician, the Friend of all — and mine also, O my Jesus!

---

[53] St. Cecilia, second- or third-century martyr and patron saint of music.

∞

Affections

O almighty Son of God, Thou didst become
man, so that men might learn to love Thee.
Sweet infant Jesus, what, then, hast
Thou come on earth to seek? Thou seekest me,
Thy poor lost sheep, that I may never wander
from Thee again and may love Thee only.

Jesus, my Treasure, my Life, my Love, my All,
accept the gift that I now make to Thee of myself.
I wish to live only to love Thee, and
I wish to die still loving Thee.

St. Alphonsus Liguori

∞

Examination of Conscience

• Have I ever seriously reflected on the love of God in
giving me His Son; on the love of Jesus in giving Himself
for me; and on the love of the Holy Spirit in forming
this wonderful union of humanity with Divinity?

• If God thus seeks me, do I allow Him to find me?

• Why do I ever fly from Him, as Adam did?
Is it because I am a sinner and love my sin?
Or is it because I do not have strength of
will to make sacrifices for His sake?

⬥ *Do I have the amount of love for Jesus
to which my state of life obliges me?*

⬥ *What shall I do henceforth to love Jesus more and
to allow Him to love me and lead me where He will?*

∾

Resolution

∾

Spiritual Bouquet

*"Our Lord wished to be born, as He was born,
because He wished to be loved."*

St. Alphonsus Liguori

Step Four

∞

Love Christ crucified

"Mount Calvary is the true school of love," says St. Francis de Sales. "Jesus hides Himself behind the wall of His humanity, and His wounds are like the lattice-work, through which His love looks at us."

Nowhere else has our blessed Savior more clearly told us how much He loves us than in those words of His: "Greater love than this no man hath, that a man lay down his life for his friends."[54] Jesus, as man, came to tell us that God loves us: we are "bought with a great price."[55]

Let us therefore fix the eyes of our soul, first, upon our loving Savior and, second, upon those happy souls who are saved.

[54] John 15:13.
[55] 1 Cor. 6:20.

∞

Christ poured out His life for your salvation

Bossuet[56] says, "Mercy and justice are like the two arms of God, but mercy is the right arm and was the first to act." When, therefore, did mercy begin to act? Before the dawn of time in the eternal ages: "I have loved thee with an everlasting love,"[57] said Almighty God to His chosen people, speaking by the mouth of His prophet. This is why He has at last given to us — to each one of us individually — life and a heart, as a precious vessel to receive His gifts of nature and grace, until we are fitted to receive His choicest gift of glory; and all these are gifts of His love.

Man, alas, would not allow himself to be guided by God's hand of mercy. He sinned against light; he sinned while he was surrounded by God's love. And then, that other arm of God was lifted up to punish the sinner. The just Judge was ready to strike the guilty offender, but God is always a Father and had compassion on the creature who was His child.

[56] Jacques Bénigne Bossuet (1627-1704), Bishop of Meaux.
[57] Jer. 31:3.

Justice must be satisfied, but the hardest part of the punishment was not borne by sinful man: another Victim — man, to be able to suffer; and God, to be able to expiate sufficiently; God-Man, to be the Mediator between God and man — bore the whole weight of the divine vengeance. Christ humiliated, Christ suffering, Christ dying — here was superabundant satisfaction to divine Justice: God annihilated before God.

Therefore, our Savior took upon Himself the sins of the whole world, from the Fall of Adam even to the last crime committed by the last man, before this world comes to an end forever. Therefore, "God spared not even His own Son, but delivered Him up for us all."[58] After thirty years of a hidden life of labor, after three years of preaching and works of mercy, we behold Him in the Garden of Olives, agonizing under the weight of our sins and the justice of His Father, and overcome with terror and grief, "exceedingly sorrowful even unto death."[59] He is betrayed by one disciple, denied by another, forsaken by all. He is buffeted and struck, condemned to a punishment reserved for slaves, beaten

[58] Cf. Rom. 8:32.
[59] Cf. Matt. 26:38.

with rods, and crowned with thorns. His body is nothing but one wound, and yet He is forced to carry His Cross. He goes to Calvary. He is nailed to the Cross between two thieves. His Father has forsaken Him. He utters one bitter cry of mortal agony. He dies. He is dead.

"The Divinity was hidden during the whole of our Savior's Passion and abandoned the most Holy Humanity, which was united with it, to the cruelest of torments," says St. Ignatius. "If we reflect on the tortures which this divine Martyr endured for us in His Heart and soul, how is it possible for us not to be moved, on beholding the innumerable agonies and incomprehensible sufferings of our Lord and Savior, Jesus Christ?" Now, when Jesus was thus "made sin for us," He "blotted out the handwriting that was against us . . . fastening it to the Cross,"[60] and eternal life was restored to us.

"See the many proofs of love that our Lord has given us, by laying down His life for us," says St. Teresa. And St. Bernard says, "If we owe Him so much gratitude for our creation, how much more do we owe Him for the wonderful way of our redemption!"

[60] 2 Cor. 5:21; Col. 2:14.

∽

Christ's Passion will lead you
to love Him more deeply

There are some persons who never pay their debts, because they are afraid of poverty. Jesus has paid all our debts, but at what a price! At what a humiliation of Himself! The smallest of His actions would have sufficed for our ransom, because everything He did was of infinite value.

But He knew that this would not be sufficient to make Him "like His brothers,"[61] and therefore He chose the kind of redemption that "He thought would be most capable of touching their hearts," says St. Robert Bellarmine.[62]

"When Joseph appeared to his brothers clothed in purple and surrounded by all the pomp of the pharaohs, he was only a noble and powerful stranger to them; but when the son of Jacob threw himself into their arms with tears in his eyes, crying out, 'I am Joseph your brother,' at once they recognized that he was of their

---

[61] Cf. Heb. 2:17.

[62] St. Robert Bellarmine (1542-1621), cardinal and theologian.

own blood. It is thus that we mortals recognize Jesus Christ, our Brother. Weak and small, as we all are at first, He comes to our arms, and as we kiss His little hands, frozen with cold, as we see Him growing up, getting older and stronger, living as a mortal, feeling, weeping, and suffering; as we contemplate His wounds, His blood, His lifeless body, we can no longer doubt the truth of these mysteries, which have made God, in very deed, our Brother."

"But oh, how much His benefits to us have cost Him!" says St. Ignatius. "For, when He prepared Himself to act according to the dictates of His love, it seems as if He must have forgotten, according to our way of speaking, that He was God. He dispossessed Himself of His felicity, which is infinite, to make us participators in it, taking upon Himself our miseries, so that He might lift the burden of them from our shoulders. He was willing to be sold into slavery, so that He might redeem us; to submit to infamy, so that we might be glorified; to die in the disgrace and torments of a criminal, so that we might have immortal life and the felicity of Heaven. Certainly, that man must be ungrateful beyond conception, and his heart must be utterly rebellious, who remains cold and unaffected by all this, and who does not see that he is under an obligation to devote himself to the honor and glory of Jesus Christ."

It is from the remembrance of the Passion of our Savior, His wounds, His Cross, and His death that the saints derive their passionate love for Christ. Whenever St. Teresa looked at her crucifix, the sight produced the tenderest words of love, and the purest ecstasies.

∞

Affections

O my soul, look upon this God-Man, crucified for thee. . . .
See how He stretches out His arms to welcome thee,
how He bows down His head to give thee the kiss of peace,
how His side is open to receive thee!

What sayest thou? Does not a God so good,
so loving, deserve to be loved?

O my Jesus, my Lord and my God,
how could I ever have forgotten Thee?
How could I have loved any other thing but Thee? . . .

O Passion of Jesus,
O Love of Jesus,
let the sweet remembrance of Thee
live forever in my heart.

St. Alphonsus Liguori

∽

Examination of Conscience

* *Do I ever think of all that I have cost Jesus? Do I remember His sufferings and death, in the hour of temptation, to prevent me from sinning or, after a fall, to excite contrition?*

* *Do I realize that whoever commits a mortal sin crucifies Jesus afresh in his heart?*

* *Have I decided once and for all to love my good Savior and allow Him to save me?*

* *Do I take pleasure in telling Jesus of my sorrows, my joys, and my difficulties, in asking Him for advice and strength, in humbling myself and asking Him to forgive me?*

∽

Resolution

∽

Spiritual Bouquet

*"At the foot of the crucifix let us write,
'See how He loved us.' I think I hear,
from every one of His wounds, a voice
issuing and asking me, 'Lovest thou me?' "*

Fr. de Poulevoy

Step Five

∞

Seek union with each Person of the Blessed Trinity

The apostle St. Paul prefers to speak of the goodness of God rather than of His majesty. Ever since the Redeemer came on earth, and God "hath reconciled us to Himself by Christ,"[63] the bonds of love have been re-established between God and His privileged creatures, and our intimate relations with each Person of the Blessed Trinity have been restored to us. St. Bonaventure[64] expresses this mutual love in a few words that are good for us to meditate upon: "By the grace of God, our soul becomes, first, the child of the eternal Father; second, the spouse of Jesus Christ; third, the temple of the Holy Spirit."

[63] 2 Cor. 5:18.

[64] St. Bonaventure (c. 1217-1274), Franciscan theologian.

∞

God is your divine Father

"Behold, what manner of charity the Father hath bestowed upon us, that we should be called, and should be, the sons of God."[65] These words express our birthright to a life infinitely superior to that given us by nature. Our birth was an act of the love of God, and His intention is that we should not only serve Him as creatures, but love Him as a Father.

Our Lord continually reminded His disciples of this truth; He took pleasure in repeating over and over again that name of Father, which had until then not been perfectly revealed. "You have but one Father, who is in Heaven."[66] "You shall pray after this manner: 'Our Father, who art in Heaven.'"[67] "I go to my Father and your Father."[68]

Now, "if God is our Father," says St. Teresa, "He must be better than all the fathers in this world." "Indeed, no one can be such a Father as He is," says St. Augustine,

[65] 1 John 3:1.
[66] Cf. Matt. 23:9.
[67] Matt. 6:9.
[68] John 20:17.

and there is in Him "the ideal of all paternity, and all maternity also." "As one whom the mother caresseth, so will I comfort you."[69]

To this love of the divine Paternity, there is a responsive feeling in the human heart, which is called, in Christian language, *piety*. Piety is, as St. Thomas says, the perfection of all religious feeling: "God prefers that we should love Him as a Father, rather than simply serve Him as our Creator. By means of religion, as Christians, we adore God; by piety we love Him, without ceasing to adore Him. Religion consecrates our souls to God; piety makes our hearts entirely His. Religion presents God with faithful servants; piety gives Him loving children who look upon Him as their good Father."

This divine Paternity, this sonship of ours, requires of us a holy life, and each of us should try to be another Jesus. Let us, therefore, give to Jesus, as to an elder brother, a deep and tender love, full of veneration, but without any of that fear which freezes our souls, contracts our hearts, paralyzes us, and finally leads to discouragement. For "you have not received the spirit of bondage again in fear; but you have

[69] Isa. 66:13.

received the spirit of adoption of sons, whereby we cry, 'Abba, Father.' "[70]

∞

Jesus is your Brother and your soul's Spouse

St. Paul calls Jesus Christ "the firstborn among many brethren."[71] And our divine Savior Himself was pleased to call us *brethren,* in the person of His Apostles. "Go," He said to the holy women at the sepulcher, "tell my brethren that I am risen from the dead."[72] "Since we are the sons of God," says St. Augustine, "Christ is indeed our Brother, both by His Father and His Mother — when He said, 'After this manner, therefore, pray: Our Father, who art in Heaven'; and when He gave Mary His Mother to us, by saying to all Christians, in the person of St. John, His beloved disciple: 'Behold thy Mother.' " He wishes, then, that all should be in common between Him and us, and that we should be friends.

But we may go farther still into this mystery of divine condescension. God has indeed desired to contract with

[70] Rom. 8:15.
[71] Rom. 8:29.
[72] Cf. Matt. 28:10.

us every possible relationship belonging to our family life. "It is St. John," says Bossuet, "who has disclosed to us a new character in Jesus Christ, the sweetest and closest of all — that of the Bridegroom of our souls. He espouses souls to Himself, loading them with gifts and filling them with pure delights; taking pleasure in them, giving Himself to them; giving them not only all that He has, but also all that He is."

Often in the Gospel, our Savior calls Himself the Bridegroom.[73] And because this name is so consoling to us, and so sweet to Him, our Savior has taken pleasure in thus manifesting Himself most often to His chosen souls.

Now, in all that we have been studying, the end is the same: Christ is the Bridegroom, and He wishes to be loved. The soul that is truly His spouse has but one thought, one love, one word, and one motive for all its actions — and that is Jesus. "He desires to be loved by us, and to love us, with a love so passionate, so tender, that it can only be expressed by the sweetness of that name of Spouse," says St. Teresa. "He asks for all our love and all our heart."

[73] Cf. Matt. 9:15, 25:1 ff.

Let us reflect carefully and see whether our heart has really given to Jesus all that is expressed by these names of *brother* and *spouse*, all that they imply of simplicity, fidelity, tender affection, and devotion.

∞

You are a temple of the Holy Spirit

"I will ask the Father," said our Lord and Savior, "and He shall give you another Paraclete, that He may abide with you forever."[74]

Creatures ask for created gifts; Jesus prays, and the answer to His prayer is that we receive the gift of the Holy Spirit. The Holy Spirit, therefore, comes to us as the gift of Jesus. He comes also of Himself, "to pour forth in our hearts the charity of God,"[75] for He is the sweetness of the Father and the Son, and He pours out upon all creatures His generous and fruitful gifts.

"The Spirit of God," says St. Paul, "dwells within you, and your bodies are the temples of the living God."[76]

[74] John 14:16.
[75] Cf. Rom. 5:5.
[76] Cf. 1 Cor. 3:16.

Seek union with each Person of the Trinity

Therefore St. Cyprian[77] says, "Be very careful to live as
becomes those whose bodies are the temples of the Holy
Spirit, so that everyone may perceive that God is indeed
dwelling in you."

Who, in our days, considers such truths as these? The
Holy Spirit — He who is the "Maker of saints" — is almost unknown among us. He loves us, as the Father and
the Son love us; He loves us as His temples.

We ought to love the Holy Spirit because He is God.
We ought also to love Him because He is the Primeval
Love, substantial and eternal. Nothing is sweeter than
love. We ought to love Him all the more because He
has loaded us with blessings."[78]

Also "the Church supplicates and addresses Him
by the sweetest names: Father of the poor, Giver of all
grace, Light of our hearts, Best of Comforters, Sweet
Guest of the soul. And she implores Him to give those
who trust in Him the merit of virtue, a happy death,
and everlasting joy."[79]

---

[77] Possibly St. Cyprian (d. 258), Bishop of Car-
thage. — ED.

[78] Pope Leo XIII, *Divinum Illud Munus*.

[79] Ibid.

∾

Affections

*Help me to understand, O my divine Master,
the ineffable greatness of my baptized soul!
God within me, my Redeemer within me,
the Holy Spirit within me!*

*O Jesus, how true it is that Thou art the good God,
in whom are all riches and all treasures!*

*Spirit of Love, come and penetrate my understanding,
so that the pure light of Jesus may shine there!
Take possession of my will, so that the holiness of
Jesus may reign there! Take possession of my heart,
and bathe it in the pure love of Thee! Take possession of
my whole being, so that therein may be manifested
the life of Jesus, my King, my Life, and my Love.*

∾

Examination of Conscience

✦ *Am I really a child of the good God in my actions, my feelings,
my thoughts, and my words? Do I give to Him the respect,
the love, and the simplicity of a child toward his Father?*

✦ *Jesus is the Brother of my soul. Do I resemble Him in any way?*

✦ *Jesus is the Bridegroom of my soul. Do I love Him?
Do I trust Him? Am I devoted to Him?*

Seek union with each Person of the Trinity

• *The Holy Spirit dwells within me. Is everything within me —
mind, heart, and body — pure? Am I determined to cast out, to
destroy, to expiate, and to purify everything that makes my soul
unworthy to be the dwelling place of the three divine Persons?*

∞
Resolution

∞
Spiritual Bouquet
*How sweet it is to abandon ourselves to the
love of God, Father, Son, and Holy Spirit.*

Step Six

∞

Stand in loving awe of God

Some exaggerate the justice of God, but the true doctrine on this point is that of St. Thomas: "I fear God
because He is just; I love Him because He is good; my
soul is lost in the thought of His sweetness."

Therefore, first, we must not be afraid of God,
and second, we must see that true fear of God leads
to love.

∞

You must not be afraid of God

"Ever since the curse which was pronounced upon
us after the Fall of man," says Bossuet, "there remains
in the human mind a certain fear of divine things which
does not allow us to approach God with confidence and
terrifies us at the idea of anything supernatural." Many
voices call to timid souls as if from God, "Adam, where

art thou?"[80] And they fly at once, hide themselves, and tremble with fear. It is this fear which keeps them from all pious practices, especially from Holy Communion. St. Gertrude says of such souls that they are afflicted with trembling paralysis.

"God is always good in Himself," says Tertullian.[81] "It is we alone who compel Him to make use of the severity of His justice."

Extreme fear leads to estrangement, not to love. "Love does not desire slaves or convicts; we are not drawn to God by chains of iron, like bulls and buffaloes, but by bands of loving kindness and a sweet attraction that gains the human heart."[82]

Instead of narrowing souls, we must give them free expansion. Fear ends in sadness, distrust, and discouragement; love produces generous devotion and inspires heroic sacrifices. Jesus wishes to be loved above all things. He is all goodness; He prefers boldness to the least sign of fear. Our thoughts of perfect trust in Him give Him more honor than any other thoughts.

[80] Cf. Gen. 3:9.

[81] Tertullian (c. 160-c. 225), African Church Father.

[82] St. Francis de Sales, *Treatise on the Love of God*.

∞

True fear of God will lead you to love

"We ought to value highly a right fear of the Divine Majesty," says St. Ignatius. "Even servile fear, when a man is unable to raise himself to anything better or more useful, helps him very much in his attempt to give up mortal sin; when that is accomplished, he easily goes on to filial fear."

As the result of this filial fear, the Holy Spirit makes us a special gift, which helps us to practice the childlike respect and loving submission that we owe to God as our Father and which makes us fly at once from sin, because it displeases Him. We have a much higher motive than that of a slave, who fears punishment from his master; one far above that of a hireling, who fears only to lose his reward. We are the children of a loving Father. We do not suffer from "the agonizing fear of being damned, or of losing Paradise," according to St. Francis de Sales. "We fear only to displease our Father, who is so kind, so sweet, and so amiable. This is a fear so mixed up with perfect trust in Him that it becomes pleasant."

"The fear of the Lord is the beginning of wisdom";[83] but the perfect flower of wisdom, "the fulfilling of the

---

[83] Ps. 110:10 (RSV = Ps. 111:10).

law, is love."[84] If we have this loving fear, we are responding to the intentions of our good God; our redemption is sure, and our abiding refuge is the Heart of our divine Master. The true God, the God who is known to our inmost soul, is a God whom it is impossible to fear. I may fear to offend Him, but above all things, I wish to be, in the words of St. Francis de Sales, "the slave of His love."

Such a God as this I know already. I have already seen Him in the mirror of my soul, wherein His image is reflected. He is my God, and I love Him. This was how Jesus appeared during the days of His life on earth — to his holy Mother Mary, to the shepherds, to St. John, and to the Magdalene — always merciful, always gentle, and always loving.

St. Francis of Assisi said, "If we knew God as the angels know Him, we would love Him as they do." The more Infinite Goodness is known, the more He is loved. The words of St. John are very true: "He that loveth not knoweth not God."[85]

Nevertheless, in this life, we can only catch some faint and fleeting glimpses of God's sweet and lovely

[84] Cf. Rom. 13:10.
[85] 1 John 4:8.

face. Nothing can really express Him but these words:
"God is charity."[86]

∽

Affections
*Make us, O Lord, to have a perpetual fear and
love of Thy holy name, for Thou never failest to
help and govern those whom Thou dost
bring up in Thy steadfast love. Amen.*

Roman Missal

∽

Examination of Conscience
* *Do I have the fear of God in my soul?*

* *Do I try to fear sin, by considering all that renders it so
detestable: its intrinsic hideousness, the Hell which it deserves,
and, above all, the offense it gives to my good God?*

* *Do I have the spirit of holy fear sufficiently?*

* *What is my attitude with regard to prayer, behavior
in church and carefulness to avoid all occasions of sin?*

* *Do I not sometimes forget that I have a right to liberty
and confidence in God and that I should have great delicacy*

[86] Ibid.

of conscience? How is it with me in reality? Am I cowardly in correcting my faults and making the necessary sacrifices, so that I may be worthy of the love of God?

∞

Resolution

∞

Spiritual Bouquet
"The more wretched we are, the more God is honored by our trust in Him."

St. Claude de la Colombière

Step Seven

∞

Recognize Christ's love in the Eucharist

"It is a law of friendship," says St. Thomas, "that we delight in living with our friends." Jesus instituted the sacrament of the Holy Eucharist so that He might obey this law of His Heart.

At the end of His Last Supper, He said to His friends, "Do this for a commemoration of me."[87] The one thought of Jesus during those last hours was to remain with us, to continue His life as man on earth, in the midst of us, and within us. This Love of all loves desired to preserve the same friendly communion with us all as He had enjoyed with His Apostles and other devoted followers. Therefore, in His mind, the Eucharist is now, as it was then, first, the sacrament of remembrance and, second, the sacrament of union.

[87] Luke 22:19.

∞

The Eucharist makes Christ ever present

"The whole of religion," says Lacordaire,[88] "is contained in one great idea: the abiding presence of God with men. Emmanuel, God with us — this is religion."

Now, one of our greatest infirmities is to forget. The pain of friendship is absence. "We do not long remember those whom we see no more," says the holy author of the *Imitation*. Absence weakens and, finally, if it is prolonged, kills the tenderest affections and ruins the closest friendships. This is why our Lord Jesus Christ wished to perpetuate the mystery of His presence and leave us a memory of Himself as long as this world shall last. Deeply rooted as were the traces of His sojourn here below, touching and dear to every soul as His life had been, forgetfulness might soon have overshadowed the fickle memory of men.

Nothing can really replace the beloved friend but himself. Well did our dear Lord know this! If He had left us no other pledge of His great love than Bethlehem and Calvary, how quickly would we have forgotten Him!

[88] Henri Dominique Lacordaire (1802-1861), French Dominican preacher.

He waited until the moment came to say farewell and then instituted the most holy sacrament of the Eucharist, as the greatest proof of His love for us. He was leaving His disciples, and He said to them, "Take this greatest of gifts, and keep it in remembrance of me." This gift was not a figure of Himself, not an object consecrated by His touch, not a portion of Himself. It was He, whole and undivided; it was Jesus in the form of the Host. "If He did great and wonderful things for us in His Incarnation, to show His love," says Bossuet, "what has He not done for us in the Holy Eucharist, the consummation and crown of all His gifts, by which He gives Himself, not in a general way to humanity, but to each faithful soul individually." He is there so that love may endure forever, and henceforth the Eucharist has become the center of all hearts; as a memory or a hope, it is the all in all of the Christian heart.

∞

The Eucharist unites you with Christ
"Having loved His own who were in the world, He loved them unto the end."[89] St. Thomas explains, "This

---

[89] John 13:1.

does not mean unto the end of His life, but unto the end of His love." And that means forever and ever.

"The peculiar attribute of intense affection between two friends," St. Thomas tells us, "is that they should live together and arrive at such a degree of union that the two lives are as one." "That they all may be one, as Thou, Father, in me and I in Thee; that they also may be one in us; I in them, and Thou in me, that they may be made perfect in one."[90]

"The Eucharist is not only God *with* us," says St. Cyril. "It is God *in* us; we become one and the same body and blood with Jesus Christ."

"The Savior blends Himself with us," St. John Chrysostom[91] tells us. "He unites His soul and body, and all that He is, with us, in order that we may be united to Him, as a body is united to its head. I say that this union surpasses all others and that, of two persons, there remains but one."

As a matter of fact, there is no union greater than that between ourselves and our food, which is changed

[90] John 17:21, 23.

[91] St. John Chrysostom (c. 347-407), Bishop of Constantinople.

into the substance of the man who takes it; and when we receive Christ, we are truly changed into Him and made one with Him. Holy Communion is the closest union that is possible to conceive; it is the ultimate degree of union, in this world; and glory is the crown of it.

"The Eucharist is to us the explanation of all the words of love, intimacy, and union that are spoken by Jesus Christ to His Church, by the Bridegroom to His Bride, by Himself to us," Bossuet tells us. Men may love each other, they may be faithful friends, but their souls are always separated. There are always, in our souls, depths into which no one can penetrate. But in the Holy Eucharist, there is nothing between the soul of Jesus and our soul. His body is united to our body, His Spirit to our spirit.

This is a supreme overflowing of the goodness and love of God; this is perfect union. "It was a great thing for our Lord to become our Companion," St. Thomas says. "It was a greater thing to become the Redeemer of our souls; but the greatest of all, the very crown of love, was to give Himself as our Food."

Jesus Himself can do no more. He has loved us unto the end.

∽

Affections

O Bread of Heaven, which, under Thy appearances
dost conceal my God whole and entire, I love Thee,
I adore Thee, my dearest Treasure.

O Jesus, O Bond of Love, which unitest the poor slave to
his Lord, if I were to live without loving Thee, I would wish
to live no longer. O my most cherished Possession, who dost
draw me to Thyself, I give Thee my heart. O my sweetest Love,
I will be forever Thine. Wait for me in Heaven; He who has given
Himself to me here can never refuse me the gift of Paradise.

St. Alphonsus Liguori

∽

Examination of Conscience

♦ *What place does the Holy Eucharist hold in my life,*
in the life of my heart and my exterior life?

♦ *Do I employ the time of Holy Mass in reviving within myself*
the remembrance of Jesus and establishing myself in His love?

♦ *Are my visits to the Blessed Sacrament as much a duty*
to me as other visits of interest, politeness, or friendship?

♦ *Do my thoughts often turn toward the tabernacle? Do I go*
there when I am tempted, or troubled, or in difficulties? Do I really
love Jesus — Jesus in the Sacred Host — with my whole heart?

Recognize Christ's love in the Eucharist

∽

Resolution

∽

Spiritual Bouquet
*"The love of the Holy Eucharist
is to live with Jesus, in the most simple,
loving, familiar, and tender manner."*

St. Peter Julian Eymard

Step Eight

∞

Receive Communion frequently

Jesus has said: "I am the living Bread, which came down from Heaven. He that eateth my flesh and drinketh my blood abideth in me, and I in Him."[92] These words are for us, and for our consolation. Now, as to Him? "With desire I have desired to eat this Pasch with you, before I suffer."[93] We have need of Him, and in His infinite love, He has condescended to have need of us. "The perfect exercise of love is the continual desire to receive Jesus Christ," says Bossuet. "His table is spread. The guests are still wanting. But, O Jesus, Thou wilt call them!"

It is necessary for us, therefore, if we wish to be really in union with Jesus, first, to communicate for His sake and, second, to communicate for our own sakes.

[92] John 6:51, 57 (RSV = John 6:51, 56).
[93] Luke 22:15.

∞

Jesus desires union with you in Communion

The words of Jesus Himself leave us in no doubt as to His divine intentions with regard to us. On the last night of His life, He said to His disciples, "With desire I have desired to eat this Pasch with you" — i.e., make this Communion with you — "before I suffer."

To bring Himself closer to us — to unite us with Himself more completely — Jesus gives Himself to us under the form of our most ordinary food. He makes us sufficiently understand that He wishes to give Himself to us every day — "I am the Bread of Life," the daily Bread of Christian life — and He sums up His intention by telling us to pray thus: "Our Father . . . give us this day our daily bread,"[94] the bread that feeds our bodies and the best Bread of all, which feeds our souls: the Bread of Christ.

The first Christians "continued every day in the Temple, and in breaking of bread, and in prayers."[95] The Apostles must therefore have received a special command from their Lord and a recommendation of daily Communion.

[94] Cf. Matt. 6:9, 11.
[95] Cf. Acts 2:42, 46.

The desire of the Church is well expressed by these words of the Council of Trent: "The holy Council desires that at all Masses, the faithful who assist thereat should receive the Holy Eucharist." And later on, at the Council of Rheims, it was said, "For the love of God, we implore the faithful to communicate as often as possible."

"It is necessary to persuade them to approach the table of the Lord as often as possible," counseled Pope Leo XIII, "for the more we frequent it, the more abundant fruit we derive from it."

And a decree of the Sacred Congregation of the Council, ratified by St. Pius X, declares that frequent and even daily Communion is in conformity with the desire of our Lord Jesus Christ and of His Church; that daily Communion produces more abundant fruits than weekly or monthly Communion; that by frequent and daily reception of the Holy Eucharist, union with Jesus Christ is increased, the spiritual life is more abundantly nourished, the soul acquires more solid virtue, and the promise of eternal life grows stronger."[96]

[96] Decree of the Sacred Congregation of the Council, December 20, 1905.

The reason for this is that the glory of Jesus is bound up with our loving reception of Him. He said truly, after the Communion of His Apostles, "Now is the Son of Man glorified, and God is glorified in Him."[97] Holy Communion is the life of Jesus continued in our souls. It is Jesus Himself shining in the world. It is His work accepted, His mediation blessed. It is the triumph of His love: He is loved as He has loved us! Therefore, St. Thomas says, "True Communion is when we eat and when we are ourselves eaten." God hungers for souls; when we receive Him in Holy Communion, "we become the bread of God," says St. Mechtildis. It was for our souls that Jesus thirsted upon the Cross.

"Let me suffer," exclaimed St. Ignatius of Antioch, the martyr.[98] "I am the wheat of God; I wish to be ground by the teeth of the beasts, so that I may become the immaculate white bread of Christ." How many saints, how many who have known and loved God best have had the same thought! St. Bernard says, "When the Savior gives Himself to me as my food, He feeds Himself also; and His own joy is the only good thing He finds in me."

[97] John 13:31.
[98] St. Ignatius (c. 35-c. 107), Bishop of Antioch.

"Jesus has an immense hunger for us, a hunger that is never satisfied," says Ruysbroeck.[99] "He knows how poor we are; but He comes to us and makes His bread for Himself." He often said so to His saints. Thus, to St. Gertrude: "I desire thee with my whole Heart; he who prevents anyone from receiving me robs me of my joy."

∞

Receiving Communion
helps you grow in holiness

"He alone can fulfill all the duties of a Christian life who has clothed himself with Christ, and no one can clothe himself with Christ except by constantly frequenting the eucharistic table," says Pope Leo XIII. The Eucharist was instituted to restore and nourish the soul of man in all its necessities, to fortify both soul and body, and to serve as a remedy. As our bodies, when exhausted with fatigue, have need of renewing with food and rest the life circulating within them, so does the soul need something to recruit its weakness and restore its strength.

[99] Jan van Ruysbroeck (1293-1381), Flemish mystic.

What is really wanting to so many souls devoured by weariness and vexations, or simply by the emptiness of life, is this sweet Bread of the Elect, the strength of the saints, the Wine of divine joys. These poor souls forget that every living being requires food according to its nature. "Hay," says St. Cyril, "is the food for animals; bread is the food of our bodies; and Christ is the Bread of the soul."

One great mistake, on our part, is to consider Holy Communion as a reward or a crown of sanctity. Holy Communion is not a reward of virtue; the highest virtue could never merit such a gift; it is a means for acquiring virtue, strengthening us against evil, and helping us to persevere and advance in perfection. "It preserves us from mortal sin and is the antidote to deliver us from our daily faults," the Council of Trent tells us. St Ambrose says, "We take this heavenly Bread every day as a daily remedy for all our infirmities."

"Approach Christ with confidence," says St. Bonaventure. "You do not go to Him to sanctify Him, but to be sanctified by Him." St. Francis de Sales says, "There are two kinds of people who should communicate often: the perfect, because they are well disposed, and the imperfect, so that they may acquire perfection; the strong, for fear they may become weak, and the weak, that they may become strong."[100]

And St. Ignatius tells us, "One of the most admirable effects of frequent Communion is to preserve us from falling into sin, and to help those who sometimes fall through weakness to rise again; it is a more certain way of making progress to approach this Divine Sacrament often, with love, reverence, and confidence."

"He who approaches the Divine Sacrament gives more glory to God than he who keeps away from it," says St. Augustine; and so St. Thomas says, "Live so that you may be able to communicate every day."

∞

Affections
O Blessed Virgin Mary,
our Lady of the Most Holy Sacrament,
thou who art the glory of all Christian people
and the joy of the universal Church, pray for us, and
kindle in the hearts of all the faithful a loving devotion
to the Most Holy Eucharist, so that we may
be worthy to communicate every day.

[100] *Introduction to the Devout Life*, Part 2, ch. 21.

∞

Examination of Conscience

* *Do I sometimes think of the joy that my Communions give to Jesus?*

* *Am I ready to carry my heart to Him as often as possible and ask for His love in return?*

* *Do I do all in my power to communicate more often, perhaps even every day?*

∞

Resolution

∞

Spiritual Bouquet

"In Holy Communion is Thy joy and my necessity. Come to me, then. Come, my loving Savior."

St. Margaret Mary

Step Nine

∞

Love the Sacred Heart of Jesus

The Sacred Heart is our treasure. It is the refuge of poor sinners, the retreat for all the saints of God, and, for us all, the tabernacle of a tenderness without limit.

When our Lord revealed His Sacred Heart to St. Margaret Mary, He said to her, "If thou didst know how I long to be loved by men! I thirst, I am on fire with the desire of being loved!" And always that same Heart of His pursues our hearts, and always He speaks the same words to us: "Abide in my love."

Let us now consider, first, the call of the divine Heart and, second, the answer of the human heart.

∞

The Sacred Heart of Jesus loves you intensely

During one of St. Gertrude's revelations, St. John said to her, "The pulsations of the Sacred Heart of Jesus shall be a most sweet language, which shall last until the end of time, so that the world, becoming torpid and frozen on account of its great age, may be warmed and comforted by the heat of divine Love."

It was at Paray-le-Monial[101] that the tabernacle opened, and Jesus Christ showed Himself to His humble servant St. Margaret Mary under a human form. He held in His hands His own Heart, pierced with a sword. "Behold," said He to her. "Behold this Heart, which has loved men so much. My divine Heart loves men so passionately that, not being able any longer to contain the flames of its ardent love, it must of necessity reveal them."

"Loves men so passionately": those are strong words!

Jesus loves us, as God loves us, with an infinite love; He loves us also with a human love — a created, limited love, as everything human must be; but with noble affection, as a perfect man must love. This love of His of the same nature as our purest human affections:

---

[101] The Visitation Convent at Paray-le-Monial in central France is where St. Margaret Mary Alacoque received the revelations of the Sacred Heart of Jesus.

as the love of a father for his child; of a brother for his brother or sister; of a friend for a friend.

I have longed for a God who will love me as I understand love, and I find Him in the words: "He was made man for us; He took flesh for our sake." Since He has taken a heart like mine, since He has opened His Heart to me, as a token of His love, it is easier for me, like St. Ignatius, "to feel, to inhale, to taste the sweetness and the infinite goodness of the Divinity."

In His state of glory now, our Savior still remains sensible to those sweet and peaceful influences, which can cause neither trouble, nor wrong, nor disorder. Therefore — and this is my greatest consolation — whatever I give Him — my love, my sacrifices, my devotion — has an effect upon His divine Heart and can make it beat with more sweetness and throb with loving joy.

So He can receive something from me! It is nothing that can really make Him richer — I know that — but something that is a response to His great love for me.

As for Him, what is it that He has not given to me? He said, "My Heart is consumed with the desire of communicating itself to souls." It is the love of Jesus Christ which pours over all the members of His Mystical

Body[102] the graces of which He is the source. And it was to recall all this to our memories, and to announce from God a new compact of love, that Jesus made that new revelation of His Sacred Heart. St. Margaret Mary, who has transmitted to us all these appeals for our love, exclaims at last, "I have no longer any wish but for God alone and to bury myself in the Sacred Heart of Jesus."

∞

The Sacred Heart of Jesus
longs for your love

"Behold," said our Lord Jesus, "behold this Heart which has loved men so much and which, in return, has met with nothing but ingratitude from the greater part of them; do thou, at least, give me the joy of atoning for this ingratitude." He had already spoken as follows to St. Francis of Assisi: "My Heart is calling to thy heart. I am waiting for thee; make haste and come to me." But it is really to all of us that He spoke, when He said to St. Peter: "Simon, son of John, lovest thou me?"[103] It is

[102]That is, the Church.
[103]John 21:15, 16, 17.

therefore "a return of love" that our good Savior desires, so that He may convert souls to Himself.

St. Margaret Mary, his "beloved disciple," as He called her, understood this so well, that she said, among the "three tyrants" that persecuted her soul, the most powerful "was such a great desire to love the Sacred Heart that it seemed everything she saw ought to be changed into flames, so that He might be loved."

To study the Sacred Heart so that we may love it, to love it and always try to love it more, and to live in conformity with this love is what Jesus asks of us when He shows us and gives us His Heart. Sovereign justice commands our fear; the greatness of God calls for our admiration; His infinite perfection excites our adoration; but His love cries out for our love in return, and the essence of all religion is that the heart of man should be one with the heart of God, in loving union with our dear Redeemer.

Let us, then, give Jesus a love that rejoices in all His perfections; a love of preference, choosing His commandments and following His wishes above all things; a love of filial friendship, so that we may always live with Him in holy, intimate, and reverential communion of thoughts, interests, and affections.

∞

Affections

Heart of my Savior, save me.
Heart most merciful, supply
for my deficiencies.
Heart most patient, bear with me.
Heart of my Master, teach me.
Heart of my Father, govern me.
Heart of my Brother, dwell with me.
Heart of my Shepherd, guard me.
Heart of my Bridegroom, love me.
Heart of my Friend, caress me.
Heart most desirable and most
beautiful, ravish me.
Heart of my King, crown me.

St. Margaret Mary

∞

Examination of Conscience
• *Do I have devotion to the Sacred Heart?*
Do I have, in my house, or on my person,
an image of the Sacred Heart, and, if so,
what do I do to honor it?

• *Do I try to live for the love of Jesus,*
according to all the requirements
of my state of life?

Love the Sacred Heart of Jesus

❖ *Is everything in my heart given to Jesus and belonging to Him? What is there in my soul that might grieve Him, or stand in the way of His will for me?*

∾

Resolution

∾

Spiritual Bouquet
"I will try to do everything and suffer everything for the love and glory of the Sacred Heart."

St. Margaret Mary

Step Ten

∞

Let Christ dwell within you

The apostle St. Paul said, "To me, to live is Christ."[104]
This most beautiful and simple truth was familiar to the
first Christians. They called the martyr who "slept in
the Lord" by the same name as Christ — "the beloved
lamb of God" — and when a little child died, they
called him the "little lamb."

In reality, says St. Ignatius, "Christ is the life of all
those who truly live." Others may "have the name of
being alive, but they are dead."[105] It follows that the more
perfect a Christian becomes, the more Christ shines in
his soul, and even in his countenance, as often happens
with the saints. Let us now try to contemplate the life
of Christ within us and in what that life consists.

[104]Phil. 1:21.
[105]Cf. Apoc. 3:1 (RSV = Rev. 3:1).

∞

You are a member of Christ's Mystical Body

When the Word became incarnate, God did not merely give Him the beautiful body of flesh that was fed and caressed by Mary, saluted by angels, crucified by the Jews, and is now present in the Holy Eucharist and crowned in Heaven. God also gave Him a Mystical Body, the members of which are all the just — every soul that is in the state of grace. Throughout the world and throughout all the ages of time — from the little child just baptized, to the holy old man at the Vatican; from gentle Abel to the last of the elect reaped by death's scythe — every innocent or penitent human soul forms the Mystical Body of Christ.

St. Athanasius[106] said, "The humanity of Christ is the whole Church"; and to every faithful soul, grace is "the seed of God."

St. Paul tells us, "We are one and the same body with Christ. He is the Head, and you are the body. We are the members of Christ."[107] If, therefore, the just form one sole body with Jesus as their Head, they must necessarily

---

[106]St. Athanasius (c. 296-373), Bishop of Alexandria.
[107]Cf. Rom. 12:5; Col. 1:18; 1 Cor. 6:15, 12:27.

have one life in common with Him. Our Lord said, "I am come that they might have life, and that they might have it more abundantly. I am their life."[108] Every one of us who is in a state of grace may truly repeat those words of the apostle: "To me, to live is Christ; Christ lives in me."[109]

And as He has only one Heart for His Mystical Body and for His body of flesh, it is from that Heart that proceeds all the sweet and benign influences that preserve and develop His life in our souls. The Heart that is the source of life for Jesus, in His immortal life, is the same Heart that gives to my soul the life of grace; I am a branch nourished by the sap of that Vine which feeds all life that exists.

"Our sweet Jesus is therefore always the Heart of our hearts," says St. Francis de Sales. Our Savior clearly expressed this truth to St. Mechtildis, when He said to her, "I will give thee my eyes, that thou mayest see all things through them; my ears, that thou mayest understand by them; my mouth, that thou mayest accomplish by it all thou hast to speak, to pray, or to sing. Finally, I

[108]Cf. John 10:10, 14:6.
[109]Phil. 1:21; Gal. 2:20.

give thee my Heart, that thou mayest think with it, and mayest love me, in all things, for myself alone." And to St. Margaret Mary He said, "I clothe thee with the robe of innocence; thou shalt henceforth live the life of the God-Man; I am thy life; thou shalt live no longer but in me and by me."

Our own humble and insignificant lives will assume infinite proportions if we spend them in living the life of Christ.

∞

You must remain united to Christ

The first and indispensable condition of the existence and permanency of the life of Jesus within us is that we should be in a state of grace. "I am the true vine," said our Lord. "You are the branches. If the branch abide not in the vine, it cannot bear fruit of itself. He that abideth in me, and I in him, the same beareth much fruit: for without me you can do nothing."[110]

When we are united to the divine Vine, all holy thoughts that present themselves to our minds, all pure affections that awaken in our hearts, all our virtues, and

[110]Cf. John 15:4-5.

all our good works are the effect of that life-giving sap of His grace, which comes from Him to us, taking root in us, springing up in our souls, working within us, and bearing much fruit. "The root of life is in God," St. Cyril tells us, "and everything springs from that root."

A member that is separated from the body no longer receives from it either life or movement. Therefore the sacred text continues: "Every branch in me that beareth not fruit, [my Father] will take away. . . . He shall be cast forth as a branch and shall wither; and they shall gather him up and cast him into the fire, and he burneth."[111]

The sinner is in a state of separation from Jesus Christ; he no longer receives any sap from the Vine; he no longer drinks the blood of his God; he is dead. The soul is dried up; charity, which, says St. Ignatius of Antioch, is "the blood of Christ," can no longer reach it; it becomes insensible to all the beauties of faith, the consolations of hope, and the attractions of the divine work. Gradually it loses the spirit of prayer, the love of virtue, the taste for devotion, and the zeal for its own salvation. And let us attentively consider these words of St. Augustine: "There is no second chance for the

[111]John 15:2, 6.

branch: either it must be united to the Vine, or it must be cast into the fire."

"If the branches of the Vine, the members of Christ's Body, could realize how much they owe to their Root and Head, they would never cease thanking Him," says Bossuet. "The crown of all their joy is that the Root takes as much pleasure in communicating His life to them as the branches take in receiving it. The Head is made to communicate with His members; it is the joy of Jesus to give Himself to us."

"Love has two effects," St. Thomas says. "It has, it holds, it possesses, and it shields within itself the person it loves, to make him rich, to give him joy and happiness; then that person, in return, walks, remains quiet, and reposes in the one he loves, and enjoys with him the gifts made to him, until at last the happiness of both is bound up in each other."

This is true union: one thought, one love; two separate beings performing the same actions.

∞

Affections

O most Blessed Virgin, obtain for us this grace,
thou who didst merit that thy Son should be born as truly

Let Christ dwell within you

in thy holy heart as from thy most chaste womb,
thou who canst say with the eternal Father, "In me is the
source of all life": produce in us this beloved Son of thine;
give Him to our hearts. Consider not how unworthy
we are of such a gift; consider only the desire
that He has to live this new life within us.

∽

Examination of Conscience

• *Do I do my utmost to keep my soul in a state of grace? Am I*
ready to sacrifice everything, even life, rather than offend God?

• *What do I do to preserve the life of Jesus within my soul?*

• *How is it with my prayers, other pious exercises, and*
watchfulness over self? In the life of my mind and heart, is
there anything that does not really agree with the life of Jesus?

∽

Resolution

∽

Spiritual Bouquet
"To me, to live is Christ,
and to die is gain."

Philippians 1:21

Step Eleven

∞

Let Christ's life grow within you

"Christ was born," says St. Augustine, "but did He remain a child? No, He grew up, He became a youth and then a perfect man. Let us, therefore, grow — rather, let Christ grow within our souls, by faith, love, and good works." Everything that has life is destined to develop and to grow. Christ dwells within us; therefore, He must continue to grow there; it is a law for Him, as for every living creature. Let us try to fathom these truths, which contain so many important lessons — first, that Christ wishes to grow within our souls and, second, that we can help Him to grow there.

∞

Christ wishes to grow in your soul

We must grow, says the apostle St. Paul, "until we all attain to the unity of the faith and of the knowledge of the Son of God, to mature manhood, to the measure of the stature of the fullness of Jesus Christ . . . from whom the whole body, joined and knit together . . . makes bodily growth and upbuilds itself in love."[112]

The Mystical Body of Christ, of which we are members, must always go on growing. There are a certain number of human beings to be created, a certain number of elect to be sanctified; there is to be at last a certain number of virgins, saints, and holy women. Each individual of the elect adds to the accidental glory of Christ: some are patterns of His strength, others of His gentleness; some display His mercy, some His eminent purity. And the more numerous the saints are, so much the more is Christ made manifest to the world, and so much the more is His kingdom increased.

In each individual Christian, Christ is also formed and grows within his soul. "Our whole life consists in being perpetually made and perpetually perfected by God," we learn from St. Augustine. The apostle St. Paul says also, "Be zealous for that which is good, my little children . . . until Christ be formed in you."[113] A

[112]Eph. 4:13, 16 (Revised Standard Version).
[113]Gal. 4:18-19.

Christian is a second Christ, the adopted son of God, and, like his eldest Brother, he ought to grow in the sight of God and man.

This is why Christ is born in our souls, and grows and becomes stronger with us. He is born within us by Baptism; He develops within us when, being united to God, as the branch to the Vine, by love and friendship, we reproduce more faithfully His life in our life.

Therefore, there is for each one of us — for every one of the members of Christ's Mystical Body — a growth of soul predestined by Providence, so that every individual soul has its proper place in the harmonious structure of the whole Body. This is finally decided when we die. "The path of the just as a shining light goeth forward and increaseth even to the perfect day."[114]

It sometimes seems as if good men die too soon or too late. This may come from the malice of sin, even venial sin, and from infidelity to grace. Mortal sin ruins us, but even slight faults hinder the growth of Christ within our souls. Origen says, "In a soul which is holy and just, Jesus grows and increases from day to day; it becomes, indeed, the mirror of His grace, wisdom, and

[114]Prov. 4:18.

virtue. In the soul of the sinner, Christ grows weaker and weaker, and finally dies."

Hold fast to "the Head, from which the whole body . . . groweth into the increase of God."[115] This is indeed a doctrine full of consolation and encouragement. When I labor, I labor in union with my beloved Lord Jesus Christ. He is such a real Friend of mine, we love each other so much, that everything is in common between us, and the growth of my soul is also His life and His expansion. What thought could possibly give me more strength and joy? The work I have to do for Him in the world will be all the more fruitful and beautiful, the more I see Him shining through my whole life.

∞

You can help Christ grow in your soul

"That we may grow up to Him in all things who is the Head, even Christ."[116] Everything can help us to "grow up" in Jesus, and develop His life within our souls — every act of virtue. But there are some things that are the basis of all others.

[115]Col. 2:19.
[116]Eph. 4:15.

First, we must open our souls to the influence of this divine life. The arteries by which the life of Christ is infused into our souls are prayer and the Sacraments. The Christian who prays early in the morning, the moment his daily life begins, opens his soul to the influences of the divine Spirit. The soul who prays well attracts the mysterious waters of grace. The soul who ten times during the day, or thirty times, remembers the "spiritual bouquet" of his meditation, in that turning toward our Lord which is the essence of a life of prayer, or who simply tries to live for Him alone, and speaks to Him in frequent brief prayers, will quickly attain to a life of union with our divine Lord. Jesus will grow in him and will communicate to him all the riches of His grace until he is perfectly united to the Source which is supremely rich in all good gifts.

This life is renewed in the sacrament of Penance, and in the Holy Eucharist it becomes so abundant, so intimate, that, in accordance with the words of our good Master, He is in us, we are in Him, and He becomes the principle of all our actions.

Afterward, if we wish that Jesus should grow within our souls, we must feed Him. But what food shall we give Him? He has not left to us the difficulty of making a choice. "My meat," He said, "is to do the will of my Father,"[117] and again He said, "Whosoever shall do the will of my Father who is in Heaven, he is my brother, and sister, and mother."[118]

One day our Lord appeared, under the form of a little child, to a good monk. The monk had no hesitation, when the duties of his rule called him away, to leave this sweet vision. On his return, Jesus again manifested Himself, but under the form of a young man, and said to him, "You see, my son, how I have grown during your absence, and in the same proportion I have grown in your soul, on account of your fidelity to your vow of obedience."

Our life should be one succession of acts of obedience to God. We are influenced more or less by persons and events, and this is only another way of being obedient to His will.

Finally, since Christ thus lives and grows within us, we can understand what He wishes of us and can measure His growth within our souls. Now, every one of us can remember one day, or one hour, or one solemn

[117]John 4:34.
[118]Matt. 12:50.

occasion, when Jesus appeared to us greater and more beautiful. It was on the day of our First Communion, or after a good retreat, or after having made some special confession — one of those hours granted by Divine Mercy which are never forgotten, when our union with Jesus grows in our soul. Let us recall all these the happiest of our memories, and let us consider attentively whether Christ is really still growing within us. When we make our examination of conscience every evening, we can then discover whether Christ has really grown within our souls since the day before.

∞

Affections

Leave me not alone in the school of Thy love, O my God, but watch over me, so that I may go on in the way of perfection, in Thee, by Thee, and with Thee.

Help me every day to make a new step in the knowledge and love of Thee, O my Beloved. It is not enough for me to know only a little of Thee; I desire to know Thee as Thou art in Thyself, and to love Thee tenderly, to live no longer in myself, but in Thee and for Thee alone.

St. Gertrude

∞

Examination of Conscience

• *Do I have a great horror of venial sin and of all imperfections, because they grieve the Christ who dwells within me, and prevent Him from growing in my soul?*

• *Do I really pray?*

• *Do I prepare myself seriously for receiving the Sacraments?*

• *Am I really resigned to the will of God?*

• *Do I faithfully make a daily examination of conscience?*

• *What is it that most hinders the growth of Christ within my soul?*

∞

Resolution

∞

Spiritual Bouquet

"The more I try to know Christ and to love Him, the more He grows within my soul."

St. Thomas

Step Twelve

∞

Let Christ act in your soul

"Whoever has Jesus in his heart," says St. Francis de Sales, "soon manifests Him in all his actions. . . . As the almond tree grows from the little nut, so this love of Jesus will be the mainspring of all your actions. And as He will live in your heart, He will live in all that you do. He will live in your eyes, in your mouth, in your hands." When a soul has really given himself to Jesus, he is really taken possession of by this almighty Master, and all his actions are performed in Him and by Him. Let us meditate, first, on the desire of Jesus to act within us and, second, on how we can assist this action of Jesus within us.

∞

Christ acts continuously in your soul
Our loving Savior once said to St. Mechtildis, "Live entirely for me; look upon all thy good works as

belonging to me, and not to thee; consider thyself only as the garment with which I clothe myself, to rule over thee, and to act in all thine actions."

"Jesus lives in us," says St. Fulgentius.[119] "He is not in a grave; He does not remain inactive and dead within us. He is in our souls as a sovereign Lord in His faithful kingdom, to rule over our whole life. He is there as the divine Cooperator in the work of our salvation; it is He who, for the greater glory of His Father, labors within us, without weariness or intermission and, with His own divine hands, shapes and kneads us, until our souls resemble His soul, and each one of us becomes another son of God — a new Christ, resplendent with sanctity."

In a vine plant, the stalk gives life to the branch by the infusion of the sap, which causes the leaves to bud forth, and which finally ripens the grapes. In like manner, the true Vine — who is our Lord — inspires our souls, which are His branches, with everything that can help in the work of our sanctification.

I have read with trembling those words of the Gospel, "Every good tree bringeth forth good fruit, and the

[119]St. Fulgentius (468-533), Bishop of Ruspe.

evil tree bringeth forth evil fruit,"[120] but I turn to Jesus as my refuge.

His grace is always with us. "It is God who worketh in you, both to will and to accomplish."[121] He lends us His own activity, to make ours fruitful; there is not one single moment during which God is not trying to persuade and help us to be better. He "whose will is our sanctification"[122] asks only that our will should be united to His will, that our life — that humble little rivulet — should be united to the broad current of His beautiful life, so that we may receive the crown of His goodness and reap the harvest which He has sown.

It is His divine life that constitutes the value of all our actions. We share in the life of God; we work with Him.

"Scarlet and purple and fine crimson make a very precious and royal drapery," St. Francis de Sales tells us, "but their magnificence is not on account of the simple wool: it all proceeds from the dye. It is true that the

[120]Matt. 7:17.
[121]Phil. 2:13.
[122]Cf. 1 Thess. 4:3.

good works of good Christians merit Heaven, but it is not because they proceed from us, and are the wool spun from our hearts; it is because they are dyed with the blood of the Son of God."[123] Thoughts, desires, and actions — everything in us assumes infinite proportions, because everything is impregnated with the virtue of the Most High and transformed by His divine influence.

In those who are really united to Him, as St. Ephrem[124] tells us, "He Himself issues from every door of their souls and bodies. Jesus Christ is in their brain, their heart, their breast, their eyes, their hands, their tongue, their ears, and their feet. And what does this divine Savior do there? He puts everything right that is wrong. He pours new life into that soul. He lives in that heart. He listens in that brain. He is the life of that breast. He sees with those eyes. He speaks with that tongue. He rules supreme in that soul."

What treasures I lose, or what merits I gain, in proportion as I act with my Savior or separate myself from Him and from the power of His virtue!

---

[123]*Treatise on the Love of God,* Bk. 11, ch. 6.

[124]Possibly St. Ephrem (c. 306-373), Syrian biblical exegete and ecclesiastical writer. — ED.

∞

You can assist Christ's action in your soul

To be really holy, we must first of all "be taught of God,"[125] and we must valiantly resist our evil nature and faithfully follow the movements of grace, "trying always to keep our souls quiet and in peace, disposed to resign ourselves to whatever it is the will of God to do with us," as St. Ignatius says.

"Let every one of you look upon himself as an instrument in the hands of Jesus Christ," says St. John Baptist de la Salle.[126] The instrument remains quietly wherever it is placed and waits for the time, the hand, the will, and the requirements of the person who uses it. He employs it, if he wishes, as he wishes, when he wishes, and as much as he wishes.

We also are like a canvas waiting for the painter's hand. The divine Painter wishes for nothing so much as to come every day and every hour, to draw His divine lineaments upon our souls. Let us leave to Him the choice of the colors; let Him put in the gold as He

[125] John 6:45.
[126] St. John Baptist de la Salle (1651-1719), founder of the Institute of the Brothers of Christian Schools.

will and vary the shadows. He will paint rays so bright that the world will recognize them as His work, and He will temper the brightness with shadows enough to keep our pride in subjection, "lest we fall into the snare of the Devil."[127]

His work sometimes seems slower than we wish. But the heavenly Artist well knows what is good for our souls. In one moment, He imprinted the image of His sacred face upon the veil of Veronica; and His work within my soul will make rapid progress if I let Him do what He will there — if I mortify the "old man"[128] without mercy, and if I accept and follow every impulse of His grace in all its fullness.

"The thought which consoles me most," says St. Margaret Mary, "is that the Sacred Heart will do everything for me if I allow Him to do as He pleases: it is His wish, His good pleasure, His desire, His work, to supply for all my defects." Jesus will do everything within me, if only I will say to Him in all sincerity, and with a firm will, "Yes, Father, for so it hath seemed good in Thy sight."[129]

[127]Cf. 1 Tim. 3:7.
[128]Eph. 4:22.
[129]Luke 10:21.

This will of ours must be active: we must cooperate with our Savior, and labor with Him. His grace will go before us, but He will not act without us.

St. Peter Damian[130] enters into particulars with regard to all our actions done with our Lord: "Let Christ be always your beloved Guest. Let Him sit at your table and share with you His delicious food. Speak to Him in sweet and friendly conversation. Keep Him in your mind. Let Him rest in your heart. Perform all your actions in union with Him. Let Him share your burdens, and when night comes, sleep upon His breast. Let Him be the soul of your studies, your conversations, and your prayers. Let Him breathe, pray, act, and suffer with you."

Nothing will make this cooperation so easy as to substitute our Lord for ourselves, by endeavoring to strip ourselves of self and to "put on the Lord Jesus Christ."[131] In proportion as our whole life centers on Him, we come at last to forget ourselves and to see no one but "Jesus only."[132] When we pray in His name, our lips are

---

[130]St. Peter Damian (1007-1072), reformer and Bishop of Ostia.

[131]Rom. 13:14.

[132]Matt. 17:8.

His. When we kneel, it is He who kneels. When we love Him with the love that He asked His Father to give us,[133] it is His Heart that answers ours. When we suffer, we cooperate in His work of redemption.[134] When we wish to do good to others, it is He whom we give to souls.

∽

Affections

*O my divine Jesus, I offer and consecrate
to Thee my heart, with all its affections;
my soul, with all its faculties; my will, so
that it may be ever united with Thine.*

*Deign to unite my intentions, words,
and actions to Thine own, and animate them
with Thy Holy Spirit. Let nothing be done by me,
except by the influence of Thy love!*

*Grant, my beloved Jesus, that all my actions
may be so many acts of adoration, love,
and submission to Thy divine will.*

St. Margaret Mary

[133]John 17:26.
[134]Cf. Col. 1:24.

∾

Examination of Conscience
• *Are all my actions those of a real Christian? Can Jesus approve of everything in me: my manner of life, my manner of dress, my friends, my way of performing my duties?*

• *In all that I did yesterday, in all that I propose doing today, did I really act, or shall I really act, as Jesus would act? What would those who see me and hear me think of my actions — that they belonged to Jesus?*

• *Am I really living as one truly devoted to my Lord?*

∾
Resolution

∾
Spiritual Bouquet
"Act as if thou were no longer acting, but as if I alone were acting in thee."

Our Lord to St. Margaret Mary

Step Thirteen

∞

Let Christ suffer in your soul

"Christ also suffered for us, leaving us an example."[135] His Passion shows to what an extent the love of God has descended; it also shows us how our love ought to ascend to Him.

It will be sweet and strengthening for us to fathom the mystery of the Passion of Christ within our souls — first, how Jesus wishes to suffer within our souls and, second, how suffering increases the union between Jesus and the souls who love Him.

∞

Christ experiences your sufferings

The apostle St. Paul uttered these words: "I fill up those things that are wanting of the sufferings of Christ

[135] 1 Pet. 2:21.

in my flesh."[136] Strange words, indeed, these seem to us! Can anything be really wanting in the sufferings of the Redeemer of the world? To the sufferings of His mortal body, most assuredly no: these were indeed superabundant and of infinite value. He said, when He was dying on the Cross: "It is finished":[137] I have satisfied for everything; I have done all that is necessary for the redemption of sinners; I have given the utmost proof of my love; I have endured to the end.

But there was still something wanting — there still is, and there will still be — in the passion of that Mystical Body of Jesus, of which we ourselves form a part, until the last of its members, the last of His predestined, has supplied the quota of suffering proper to his state of life.

Just as, on His entrance into this world, when He offered Himself as a Victim to His Father, the divine Infant could have said to His hands and feet, "One day you will be nailed to a malefactor's Cross," in like manner, as He foresaw how His elect would in time be born and come to maturity, He understood, in His infinite

[136]Col. 1:24.
[137]John 19:30.

foreknowledge, all the details of grief and suffering which were to complete the passion of His Mystical Body. And, in proportion as trials and sorrows crucify us, we have the ineffable consolation of being able to say to our Savior, "It is Thy will to press Thy crown of thorns upon my head; so be it! It is Thy will to wound my heart with Thine agony; my heart is ready!" There is not one suffering that attacks us that cannot be made divine and sweet, through the certainty of this truth, that the God-Man repeats over us the words of a mother bending over the cradle of her beloved little one: "I suffer with my child."

"Our joy is to be partakers of Christ's sufferings."[138] "We bear in our body the mortification of Jesus."[139] "With Christ I am nailed to the Cross."[140]

When the feast of the Pasch was approaching, a few days before His death, our dear Lord spoke to His disciples of His coming Passion and of the great law of suffering that was to be the portion of His friends. Suddenly He interrupted His discourse; it seemed as if an agony

[138]Cf. 1 Pet. 4:13.
[139]Cf. 2 Cor. 4:10.
[140]Gal. 2:19.

similar to that of Gethsemane was overshadowing His soul, and He cried out, "Now is my soul troubled, and what shall I say — 'Father, save me from this hour'?"[141]

According to learned interpreters, He then felt in His own soul the agonies of all other sufferers. He embraced all our terrors, when we shrink from the severities of penance and the cruel roughness of the way of perfection, as afterward, in the Garden of Olives, He almost seemed to hesitate and shrink from such a prospect. But very quickly this fear yielded to the intensity of His divine love and pity, and He cried out, "Father, it was for this hour that I came. Glorify Thy name."[142]

Not wishing to deprive us of the Cross, because it is so good for us, He draws our crosses closer to His own. He Himself is to be found, deep down in our chalices of pain, so that there we may find love.

∞

Suffering unites you with Christ
In the midst of all our sufferings, Jesus comes, or returns to us, with more facility. If any man has never

[141]John 12:27.
[142]Cf. John 12:27-28.

suffered with and for Jesus, he cannot be sure that he loves Him. Jesus is ours, in every mystery of His life; nevertheless, no other mystery draws Him so closely to us as that of His Passion. The special character of His Passion is that there He seems to belong to Himself no longer and abandons Himself to everyone and everything, without making any resistance.

In the days of His public ministry, He went wherever He wished to go. He fled from His friends when they wished to make Him king and from His enemies when they were preparing to stone Him. He went to Bethany later than He was expected. He became the guest of the publican without being invited. In fact, He remained His own master. But during His Passion, all this is changed. Now He is only a Lamb that is being dragged to its death, without a cry or a complaint. "They have done unto Him whatsoever they had a mind."[143]

"And if this mystery has delivered Him over to His enemies, how much more has it given Him to His friends!" says Msgr. Gay. "There are secrets which can never be told, and mutual exchanges of love which can

[143]Matt. 17:12.

only be found in the Cross. Oh, who can express what a half-hour is which is passed in the very soul of a crucifix, heart to heart with that Heart, where the fullness of the Spirit of Christ reposes? Who can express all that is revealed there, and how graces flow into the soul during such an hour with God? Suffering is a kiss from the crucifix."

It is then that we find ourselves truly with Jesus, and perhaps nowhere else does His presence seem to us so sweet, so consoling, and so tender. When one of His friends is deluded by the false joys of the world, it is suffering that calls him home. "The Cross is the rendezvous to which His love invites His chosen friends," Père Tissot said. "I have sought Thee amongst the roses of this world, saying, 'Is the divine Heart here?' But the flowers were silent. Then Thine own divine hands led me trembling into the midst of thorns and briers, and Thou didst say to me, 'I am here!' " It was thus that, one day, the seraphic Francis of Assisi, kneeling before the crucifix, saw his divine Lord bend down from the Cross and press him to His Heart.

It is one of the conditions of such favors as these — such real friendship between God and ourselves — that we must, as St. Ignatius says, "grieve with Jesus Christ, in our own griefs; our souls must be broken with Jesus Christ, as His soul and body were broken."

St. Rose of Lima said to our Lord, "O my Beloved, I will keep for Thee the secret of my tears; Thou alone shalt see them flow." We sometimes complain that our dear Lord does not console us — that His Heart says nothing to us. Is there anything to be astonished at? We come to Him after we have poured out the perfume of our sufferings to creatures, and when at last we come to Him and tell Him of them, it is as if we offered Him a bouquet of faded flowers, which has already passed through several hands. We must remain, as Père Tissot says, "under the winepress, united to Jesus, alone with our grief and the God who measures it out to us."

It is then that we shall begin to understand, by sweet experience, in the words of St. Ignatius, "how our Lord Jesus Christ exercises the office of Comforter to His own, as a loving friend consoles His friends."

∞

Affections

My beloved Jesus, I desire to suffer with Thee.
To bear suffering for a friend is no longer to suffer.
To love and endure all things: this is my joy. Allow me,

then, to suffer, to love Thee, and to die. Prune, cut, burn,
destroy, if it is Thy will, O blessed hand! But grant me faith,
love, and hope, O my God, so that I may see Thee in the
midst of all my pain, which is the work of Thy charity.

∞

Examination of Conscience

• Do I wish to accustom myself to the contemplation of
Jesus suffering and, afterward, to be resigned, gentle,
and patient, in the midst of the trials of each day?

• Do I accept any troubles that come to me as a means of
salvation? What a great work it would be to offer my
body, soul, and heart to Jesus as a sacrifice!

• Do I trouble others with my grievances, or is Jesus
my only confidant, or, at least, my first confidant?

∞

Resolution

∞

Spiritual Bouquet
"I have tried to bear upon my shoulder the
cross that weighs upon Thy life. Yes, I am
willing to suffer; I consent to be silent."

Père J. Tissot

Step Fourteen

∞

Keep God's commandments

The essence of sanctity is to do the will of God. It is to that will that my own will must be united, and His law must be deeply rooted in my heart. Our meeting place with God is wherever we find His will. There we are united to Him; we are in agreement with Him. We have made the first step toward His friendship, for "love is the fulfilling of the law." Let us, then, enter courageously into the way of obedience, by meditating upon these two great truths — first, that it was divine Love which gave us the commandments and, second, that it is by love that we must keep them.

∞

God's law is one of love

"It was Infinite Wisdom," Bossuet tells us, "as well as Infinite Goodness, which decreed all the precepts and counsels of perfection which are presented for our observance."

"The commands of God are more profitable to him who obeys them than to Him who has given them," says St. Prosper.[144] So man realizes his own greatness in being associated with the divine will, in becoming the auxiliary of his Creator, in entering the service of the best of Masters, and remaining the devoted son of the most amiable of Fathers. Moreover, our perfection and happiness consist in this willing service and love — so much so that St. Jerome[145] says, "It is through His benevolent love for us that God wishes to be our Master and to command us."

The divine law is a law of love. And this love increases its commands and recommendations, just as a mother, with her child, can never say enough, never be sufficiently careful, and never take enough precautions. Real friendship may be known by the constant good advice it gives, such as the advice of a friend to his friend, or of a husband to his wife. Thus, God has made His law a light to shine upon the path of the just: it is "sweeter

[144]Probably St. Prosper of Aquitaine (c. 390-c. 463), theologian. — ED.

[145]St. Jerome (c. 342-420), biblical scholar.

than honey and the honeycomb";[146] it fills the soul with an abundance of peace; it is a foretaste of beatitude.

"It is good for a man, when he hath borne the yoke from his youth."[147] Man sometimes desires to cast off this yoke and succeeds only in losing the grace that made it so sweet. He breaks the soft bands of divine assistance, and the broken remains wound his body and impede his steps. So it is in our own lives. When am I troubled and unhappy? Is it not when I have trampled underfoot the laws of my God and my Father? When is it that I am grieved, hurt, and scandalized by the conduct of my companions in exile? Is it not when they also have disobeyed the law of God?

Finally, "it is the grace of God, through our Lord Jesus Christ, which delivers us from this slavery,"[148] as St. Paul tells us. The grace that forestalls us, strengthens us, pardons us, and helps us to begin again and persevere is His wonderful love for us; and the other grace, which is His free gift, is our love for Him, which binds us so strongly to His love and service, that no threats, no

[146]Cf. Ps. 18:11 (RSV = Ps. 19:10).
[147]Lam. 3:27.
[148]Cf. Rom. 7:24-25.

promises, and no seductions can ever separate us from Him again.

Our loving Savior knows it is love that influences us, fascinates us, makes us undertake all things, and realize all things; therefore He has implanted this law in His own Heart — He has taken a human heart. And just as God assumed a human form in His Incarnation, so He reduces His law to the measure of our strength. He says, "Come unto me, all you that labor and are burdened . . . because I am meek and humble of heart. . . . Take up my yoke upon you and learn of me, and you shall find rest to your souls."[149] He assures us that the commandment to love is the first and greatest commandment, and that every other duty is included in it.[150]

Let us therefore ask of Him a perfect understanding of His precepts, that we may obey them more faithfully.

∞

Christ helps you keep God's commandments
The friends of God are called just. Now, in what does justice consist, if not in the perfect agreement of

[149]Cf. Matt. 11:28-29.
[150]Matt. 23:37-40.

two wills? Since it was through love that God gave His commandments, how can they be observed, unless it is also through love? We win our friendship with Jesus by our loving fidelity to Him. "Love requires that we should submit everything to God — our desires, and our will," says St. Francis de Sales. "In this way, we shall attain not only the faithful observance of His commandments, but the love of them."

Our Lord has said: "If anyone loves me, he will keep my commandments; and my Father will love him, and I will love him and will manifest myself to him."[151] Here is indeed a promise of friendship: I will manifest myself to him; I will make myself known to him — the very depths of my Heart, and every knowledge of me that he is capable of receiving.

Our Lord blesses and assists all those who are continually laboring to overcome themselves, who open up their souls to His divine illumination and respond to His desire of closer union with them.

Think of the love with which Jesus accomplished the will of His Father. From Heaven to Bethlehem, from Bethlehem to Calvary, it was one perpetual "So be it,

[151]John 14:21.

117

my Father," and He never ceased until He could say, "It is finished"[152] — the whole law is accomplished. Lay your hand upon His Heart: it has just stopped, and He has died by an act of perfect obedience.

What He commanded us to do, He has done Himself. His actions are now my law, and my life henceforth should be a mirror in which His life is depicted. Thus Jesus has changed the law into a tender call of love from God to man; and obedience to law is the grateful response of the love of man for God.

Well, it is this very Christ, whose meat was to do the will of His Father,[153] whom we receive in Holy Communion; and He remains within our souls, from one Communion to another, to keep us faithful to God.

A yoke usually couples two animals together, to do the same work and for the same heavy burdens. And Jesus unites Himself to us, so that He may help us to bear our burdens and labor with us in the stony fields of this life. He shares in all our duties. He helps us in all our acts of virtue and encourages us in all our efforts. With such a thought as this, in such a union, how easy

[152]John 19:30.
[153]John 4:34.

everything becomes to the soul that loves. And when He who commands us loves us also, everything hard and bitter becomes sweet.

∞

Affections

O my Savior, I adore Thee in Thy most
perfect submission to the will of Thy Father.
I ask forgiveness for all the hindrances
that I have opposed to Thy most holy will.
In union with the perfect obedience that Thou,
Thy Blessed Mother, and all Thy saints
have shown to the divine will, I wish
for nothing, in life or in death, but a
perfect resignation to Thine adorable will.

St. John Eudes

∞

Examination of Conscience

* *Am I sufficiently instructed in all the commandments of God and the Church? When I have any doubts, do I take the proper means for setting them at rest?*

* *Am I ready to die rather than offend God mortally?*

* *Am I very prudent and delicate in resisting everything that could wound my conscience?*

• *Do I carefully study the Catechism,*
so that I may be able to give sound advice to anyone
who asks me questions on religious subjects?

∞

Resolution

∞

Spiritual Bouquet
"My sweet Jesus, I choose Thee
for the King of my heart and submit myself
forever to all Thy holy laws and ordinances."

St. Francis de Sales

Step Fifteen

∞

Find union with Jesus in your vocation[154]

"We keep the commandments so that we may not displease God," says St. Francis de Sales, "but we follow the counsels of perfection so that we may please Him, and nothing makes our friendship with God so close as this fidelity.

Let us, then, meditate upon Jesus' desire for your perfection and how your perfection is to be found in your vows and your rule.

∞

Jesus desires your perfection

Our loving Savior expresses the desire of His Heart in these general terms: "Be you therefore perfect, as also

[154]This chapter is included particularly for those in religious life, but laypersons may profit from it as well.

your heavenly Father is perfect."[155] "Blessed are they that hunger and thirst after justice."[156] These words are addressed to all Christians: every Christian ought to sanctify himself and glorify God in the manner and according to the means in his power.

The tending to perfection is part of the privilege of chosen souls; it becomes an obligation and necessity for those in religion. A nun, for instance, is, or ought to be, by her vocation, a perfect woman. "I do not mean to say," said St. Francis de Sales, "that this congregation, more than any other, must be a family of perfect souls, but they must be souls which aspire to perfection. This is a school to which they have come to learn how to be perfect, and to attain this end, it is necessary that they should have a firm will to embrace every means of perfecting themselves, according to their vocation and the institute to which they are called."

St. Alphonsus Liguori says, "Jesus Christ will forgive consecrated virgins — His brides — all their faults except a want of love for Him. If a nun does not love God, who, then, can be expected to love Him? Therefore,

[155]Matt. 5:48.
[156]Matt. 5:6.

you, my good Sister, who already have been raised to the rank of His spouses, must love Him.

"Tell me: if a great prince, rich, beautiful, and amiable, became the husband of a poor village maiden, without education and without intellect or culture, and if, by marrying her, he were to make her at once rich, noble, intellectual, bright, and happy, what would she not do in her gratitude for such a husband? Would she try to understand all his wishes, in order to give him pleasure? Would she take the greatest care to obey all his commands, without the slightest hesitation or murmuring, whenever He expressed his wishes? And if it were necessary for her to suffer pain for his sake, how gladly and quickly would she accept it!

"Apply this allegory to yourself, my Sister, to you, a poor sinner, whom He has deigned to raise to the dignity of a spouse of Jesus Christ."

It is impossible for a religious soul either to love God or to attain to the union with Him that belongs to his state unless he seeks constantly to be perfect — that is to say, to satisfy all the desires of his Savior.

A wise old author has written, "If you say, 'I do not wish to be a dove, but a hen; I wish always to live on my dunghill, pecking little grains of corn and amusing myself as I please, for it is too much trouble to be a dove, to mortify oneself and continually to do violence to one's inclinations,' I would tell you that you must go elsewhere, for you can never enter and dwell within the Heart of the Savior."

I ought to be perfect, for the glory of Jesus, for my own sanctification, and also in the interests of the spiritual family that has adopted me. Let every one of us try to be a saint. It is the surest means of attracting other vocations, fulfilling the intentions of our holy founders, and honoring our order. A very little tenderness of heart will help us to understand these arguments.

∞

Perfection is found in fidelity
to your vows and your rule

"You are very happy, my children," said the holy Bishop of Geneva to his Daughters of the Visitation. "You know perfectly well what you have to do in order to become saints."

Indeed, religious men and women have very exact advice from the Savior Himself, in what is commonly called in Christian language, the *Evangelical Counsels* of poverty, chastity, and obedience, which they are obliged by vow to follow. They have, besides, their holy rule and the traditions of each institute: the way is all marked out for them. It will be more or less difficult in proportion as the love that calls them is more tender, and their answering love stronger and more trusting; but the way itself is always shining with light, always certain, always straight.

The vows of religion have often been compared to the three nails that fastened the Crucified to His Cross; they are, indeed, the sacred bonds that bind religious souls to Jesus, their Savior. But, then, is not that to say how faithful, obedient, and separated from the world they ought to be who have made such promises?

"One is not a saint because one has taken vows, but only if one faithfully keeps them," St. Francis de Sales explains. A nun who has no other desire but to remain the loving and tender spouse of her Savior should often examine her actions and her heart, to find out whether she is still detached from all things, entirely possessed by her Lord, and devoted to His wishes.

After the vows, it is the holy rule that expresses the will of God, and superiors are authorized guardians of the rule. Its faithful observance is "the shortest road to eternal salvation and sanctity," says St. Mary Magdalene de' Pazzi.[157] Fidelity to a rule is so much a proof of friendship with Jesus that the saint often repeated, "Love thy rule as much as thou dost love God Himself."

∞

Affections

When shall I be able to love Thee, O Jesus, as much as Thou hast loved me? Thou hast drawn me from the dangers of the world and placed me in Thine own house, in the midst of thy spouses. Help me, Lord, for I wish to love Thee and to do all that is in my power to please Thee. I promise Thee never again to fail in the obedience that I owe to my superiors and to observe the smallest rules of my congregation, because they are all pleasing to Thee.

St. Alphonsus Liguori

∞

Examination of Conscience

* *Do I really lead the life of a true spouse of Jesus?*

* *Is everything in me as it ought to be in a soul obliged to aim at perfection? Do those who see me — Jesus and my superiors — think this of me?*

[157]St. Mary Magdalene de' Pazzi (1566-1607), Carmelite mystic.

Find union with Jesus in your vocation

- *If I examine each of my vows,
  can I say that I am faithful absolutely?*

- *What is my attitude with regard to my superiors?*

- *Do I observe my rule with affection and fidelity?*

- *If I were summoned tonight before the tribunal of God,
  what is there that would make me uneasy?*

∽

Resolution

∽

Spiritual Bouquet
*"O Jesus, I am a religious;
I am Thy spouse.
Help me to become a saint."*

St. Alphonsus Liguori

Step Sixteen

∞

Find union with Jesus in prayer

"Our progress in holiness," says St. Augustine, exactly corresponds to our progress in the spirit of prayer: he who prays well lives well." To be real friends of Jesus, and to ask Him for everything we need with the familiarity of love, we must study the best way to pray — first, the necessity of prayer and, second, the prayer of the friends of Jesus.

∞

Prayer obtains everything

Everything is obtained by prayer. We know this, especially since we have had the promise of our Savior: "Whatsoever you shall ask the Father in my name, that will I do."[158] Perhaps humanity would never have dared

[158]John 14:13.

to ask such a grace from God or proposed an exchange so entirely in our own favor. In this, as in everything else, it is our Lord who makes the first advance.

There is both a command and a request in those words of His: "Continue in my love" — a command, because no creature is allowed to repulse the advances of his Creator, and a request, because the Heart of this good Master really addressed each one of us in the ardent appeal that He made to His beloved confidante St. Margaret Mary: "I thirst to be loved."

Some persons complain to God that He is so sparing of His gifts, that He reveals Himself so little to these persons, and that He measures out their happiness, and perhaps their holiness, with a niggardly hand. The answer of Almighty God is very simple: "*Whatsoever* you ask, you shall obtain it."[159]

Here is His justification and our condemnation. His treasures are open to us if we will stretch out our hands to receive them. It is true that, like a prudent master, He locks up the treasures destined for His friends, but He puts the key in our own hands, and it is for us to use it.

[159]Cf. Matt. 21:22.

If we reflect on the fewness of the souls who attain to this privilege of real union with our Lord, can we not discover the cause in the very limited part that prayer occupies in their lives? There is plenty of room in most lives for self-interest, petty ambitions, earthly pleasures, and all those nothings that often engross a whole existence. Prayer plays a very small part in the lives of many persons.

In the world and in religion, the holiest souls, those most united to Jesus, are always souls who love prayer and meditation. "The only reason we obtain so few gifts from God is that we do not ask for them with sufficient earnestness," says St. Claude de la Colombière.[160]

∞

Prayer calls for confidence,
familiarity, and humility

The dominant note and distinctive character of the prayer of the Savior's friends is confidence. In countries where the Faith has nearly died out, where indifference

[160]St. Claude de la Colombière (1641-1682), French Jesuit priest; spiritual director of St. Mary Margaret Alacoque.

influences the minds of men and charity has grown cold in their hearts, they keep at a distance from Christ; they stay at the back of the church and say a few timid prayers, as far away as possible from the tabernacle.

On the contrary, in countries where the Faith remains a living Faith, and the love of Christ is stronger, warmer, and more intimate, the faithful draw near the altar and wish to be as near Jesus as possible. They almost seem too bold in their desire to see this Friend; they feel at home in the home of their good God.

The saints pray with respect: what can be more respectful than love, even in its tenderest familiarities? They pray with humility: what can be more humble than love, in its faithful service, its devotion, and its joy in giving itself? They pray with perseverance, for they know that the hour will come at last when their Friend, "who chooses His own time and His own way," will smile upon them and give them their "heart's desire."[161] But over and above all these dispositions, the highest of all is perfect trust in God.

It is something marvelous. We remember the prayer of Abraham. The Lord had said, "If fifty just men can be

[161] Cf. Ps. 36:4 (RSV = Ps. 37:4).

found in the city, I will spare it." "Wilt Thou spare it, my God, if there shall lack five of the fifty? And if only forty, only thirty, only twenty? . . . O let not the Lord be angry. . . . Wilt Thou not spare it if ten shall be found there?" And the Lord said, "I will not destroy it for the sake of ten."[162]

We remember the prayer of the poor mother in Canaan, already refused by our Lord, when He said, to try her faith, " 'It is not good to take the bread of the children and to cast it to the dogs.' And she said, 'Yea, Lord, but the whelps also eat of the crumbs that fall from the table of their masters.' And Jesus said, 'O woman, great is thy faith; be it done to thee as thou wilt.' And her daughter was cured from that hour."[163]

We remember the prayer of Mary, the sister of Lazarus, when her brother was ill. She said but one word, for she well knew the Heart to which she appealed: "Lord, he whom Thou lovest is sick."[164]

St. Teresa defined prayer in general, and mental prayer in particular, as "a loving exchange of friendship

[162]Gen. 18:23-33.
[163]Matt. 15:21-28.
[164]John 11:3.

between God and the soul." She tells us also that she sometimes said "foolish things" to her heavenly Bridegroom. Ah, the boldness of this dear saint! She was praying one day for her brother, who was very ill, and she said, "Lord, if Thou hadst a brother who needed my help as much as I need Thine, how couldst Thou bear it if I left him to suffer?"

We think we are obliged to have books, to study much, and to use choice expressions and prepared speeches. This is why our prayer leaves us dry, costs us much labor, and becomes a burden. Let us make up our minds, once and for all, to consider ourselves the friends and companions of Jesus and, like St. Teresa, "to treat Him as a Father, a Friend, and the loving Bridegroom of our souls."

"The great secret," says St. Jane Frances de Chantal,[165] "is to go to our prayer in good faith and in all simplicity."

∞
Affections
*Thou art ready, O my Savior, to give me
all the graces that I ask of Thee.*

[165]St. Jane Frances de Chantal (1572-1641), foundress of the Visitation Order.

Find union with Jesus in prayer

Thou dost desire to help me to live in Thy love,
even more than I desire it myself.
O God of my soul, I wish to love Thee;
give me a holy love of Thyself, and, in order
that I may be certain of obtaining it,
grant me the gift of prayer.

O Mary, by the love thou
didst bear for Jesus Christ, obtain for me
the grace always to have recourse
to thee and to thy divine Son.

St. Alphonsus Liguori

∞

Examination of Conscience

✦ *Am I always faithful to my prayers?*

✦ *Do I pray with faith, respect, humility,*
and confidence? Above all things, with
simplicity and sweet familiarity?

✦ *Do I make my meditation carefully, every day,*
trying to take every means of making it fruitful?

✦ *Is my life a continual prayer,*
through my union with our divine Lord
and the purity of my intentions?

✦ *What is there in me that needs reforming?*

A Pocket Retreat for Catholics

∞

Resolution

∞

Spiritual Bouquet
*"Do Thou alone speak to me, Lord, and
suffer me to speak to Thee alone, as a friend
to a Friend, in loving conversation."*

Imitation of Christ, Bk. 4, ch. 13, no. 1

Step Seventeen

∞

*Let all your thoughts, words,
and actions unite you with Jesus*

Christian piety is the union of our thoughts, our affections, and our whole life with the thoughts, feelings, and mind of Jesus. It is Jesus living in our souls. Those who practice it well — i.e., really devout souls — "have wings to fly to God in prayer, and feet with which to walk with men on earth, edifying them by a holy and amiable life," St. Francis de Sales tells us.

The life of piety and union with God consists of two things: first, our exercises of piety and, second, our practice of piety.

∞

Pious exercises lead you to God

Among our pious exercises, there are some that help us to meditate and others that help us to pray. The first make us clear away all obstacles that hinder us from drawing near to our good God, such as darkness and coldness. These exercises are meditation, examination of conscience, and spiritual reading. There are others that honor God more directly and are the cries of a soul calling upon Him. These draw Him to us. Such are vocal and mental prayer, participating in Holy Mass, visiting the Blessed Sacrament, praying our Rosary, etc.

All these have a real influence in preparing us for the visits of God and for union with our loving Savior. Without these helps, our piety languishes, our heart forgets, and, being no longer at peace with God or with ourselves, we fly to creatures, try to find our happiness in them, and so forget God. St. Francis de Sales calls our exercises of piety "the little tapers of divine love." They are to the soul what wood is to the fire or food is to the body. Without this indispensable nourishment, our souls grow feeble and finally die.

How, then, can we explain the carelessness and distaste with which these pious exercises are often treated? Everything else is attended to and has its place, its day, and its hour in our lives. It is only our spiritual duties that are deferred and neglected, in the midst of worldly occupations, pleasures, and caprices.

Let all your thoughts unite you with Jesus

We are astonished sometimes that there are so few saints now, that real contemplatives become more and more rare, and that God finds so few souls with whom He can really hold close, continual, and loving communion. He is so often forsaken, and the number is so small of those who grieve to see their own lives completely taken up, frittered away, and distracted by the claims of the world. Piety is not exercised. "Souls are now only like an unfenced orchard," says St. Francis de Sales, "which offers its fruits to all the passersby, so that nothing is reserved for its real Master."

What is really wanting in them all is the root of the whole matter: the conviction that piety is the aim and end of life, and that if we wish to preserve it and encourage its growth, we must be faithful to the exercises that sustain and develop it. A soul that is in good faith will not finish this meditation without a careful examination of self, to see what is wrong and discover the means of being more faithful in the future.

∞

All your actions can unite you with Jesus

Pious exercises are not an end; they are only a means. The real end is piety itself — i.e., the love of

God and the search for Him. Many persons reverse this order of things and fall into a false piety; they soon become nothing more than what St. Francis de Sales called "statues and phantoms of devotion." They neglect the duties of their state to prolong their prayers, assist at a grand ceremony, or hear a sermon; but they have no idea of how "to unite the care of the house of their soul with that of their exterior house, nor how to accommodate their pious exercises with their domestic duties."

There is one means of compensation for those souls whose painful and absorbing duties and the requirements of their state prevent from prolonging or multiplying their pious exercises. There is the exercise of piety itself, which consists in performing all our duties in union with the will of God and offering them all to Him as an act of love.

"Everything you do is thus watered by the blessing of God," St. Francis de Sales tells us. "And the more loving is your offering, the more perfection will you attain. Do as our Blessed Lady did in the days of our Savior's infancy, when she worked with one hand and held her sweet little Baby with the other." Everything that is done as a duty of our state, everything that is necessary, everything that the divine will has imposed upon our will, becomes a real exercise of piety. "We can be saints everywhere, if we really wish to be saints," says St. Claude de la Colombière. Everywhere and in everything, if a person desires to seek, to see, to love, and to serve Jesus, he is exercising piety, whether he commands or obeys.

"No company and no difficulties can hinder our souls from being with Jesus, and with His angels and saints," says St. Francis de Sales. The devout soul knows, in the midst of all distractions, how to unite himself with his divine Master by an act of love, "like the pilgrim who takes a little wine, without stopping on his journey, simply that he may be strengthened to continue it."

Aspirations also embalm the soul, like a few grains of incense, burning every hour, that perfume the sanctuary; these prayers also make the soul, in the words of Origen, "a permanent altar where the sacrifice is perpetuated night and day."

It is true piety, amiable and apostolic, "that leaves God sometimes to make itself agreeable to its neighbor for the love of God," says St. Francis de Sales. In certain situations, it is better "that we should try to find God in all that we do," and "our duty is to regulate as well as possible the different things that are the objects of our occupation and our care," St. Ignatius tells us.

St. Margaret Mary prayed while taking care of the little ass belonging to the convent and while preparing the vegetables. Another soul, far advanced in contemplation and even sometimes rapt into ecstasy, said to our Lord, when called away by obedience for some necessary work, "No, my Jesus, not now; I cannot stay with you now."

When a soul complains that his employments distract him, that they separate him from our Lord and become an obstacle to his salvation and sanctification, he is under a delusion. Nothing is so good for him as obedience, and nothing is better for him than the office appointed by those in authority over him.

∞

Affections

O Sacred Heart of Jesus,
I give and consecrate myself to Thy love and glory.
May all that I see and hear lead me to love Thee more!
May all my words be so many acts of adoration, love, and praise!
May every movement of my lips be an act of contrition for all the
sins I have committed and all the good I have left undone!
May every step I take bring me nearer to Thee and
all my actions unite me to Thee more and more.

St. Margaret Mary

Let all your thoughts unite you with Jesus

∞

Examination of Conscience
 • *Do I perform all my exercises of piety
carefully, respectfully, and faithfully? Do I omit
or defer them, unless from necessity or charity?*

 • *Is my piety always gentle, amiable, and joyous?
Is it ever annoying to anyone and
always according to holy obedience?*

 • *Does the spirit of faith make all my
actions a perpetual exercise of piety?*

∞
Resolution

∞
Spiritual Bouquet
*"Sacred Heart of Jesus, increase
my desire to pray, to work, and
to please Thee in everything."*

St. Margaret Mary

Step Eighteen

∞

See Jesus in your neighbor

Everyone has a weak side, which most influences him and to which his will is most attached. The Heart of Jesus — let us not be scandalized — is a created Heart, capable of emotions and affections like ours, in all that is most calm and holy in them. Therefore, Christ has his "weak side," as we have, and, humanly speaking, He has His desires and wishes, which we must try to gratify if we wish to win His Heart. These are doors opened more widely, by which we can penetrate even to Him — doors that are never closed and through which He Himself prefers to come to us.

To those souls who desire to find the tenderest spot in our dear Savior's Heart, and to approach Him there, this meditation will try to reveal, first, what is the "weak side" of Jesus and, second, how we can approach Him on that side.

∞

Jesus calls you to love your neighbor

An experienced eye will soon discover what is this "weakness" of Jesus, by contemplating His conduct when on earth — His actions, His way of looking at things, His predilections, and especially His words.

Now, let us listen to some of the words of Jesus: "Thou shalt love thy neighbor as thyself."[166] "A new commandment I give unto you, that you love one another; as I have loved you, that you also love one another."[167] "This is my commandment, that you love one another, as I have loved you."[168]

Are these words sufficiently clear? Is His intention plain enough, His entreaty sufficiently expressive? Here we have a real partiality, a real desire, on His part — a command from His Heart. He insists upon it; He repeats it over and over again; He is attached to it. "Our Lord declares that it is His own commandment, His very own, the dearest to His Heart, and the most loved of all," says St. Francis de Sales. "After the command to

[166]Mark 12:31.
[167]John 13:34.
[168]John 15:12.

love God, there is no greater commandment than this love of our neighbor."

The last time our Lord said these words was on the eve of His death — a time when everything that is said makes the greatest impression upon those who are to be left and can never be forgotten. Afterward He added, "By this shall all men know that you are my disciples, if you love one another."[169] St. John said afterward, "In this the children of God are manifest and the children of the Devil: whosoever is not just is not of God, nor he that loveth not his brother."[170]

The Apostles heard and understood. They preached the gospel of love; they taught that we must love our fellowmen for the sake of God, by whom man had been created. St. Paul says, "All the law is fulfilled in one word: Thou shalt love thy neighbor as thyself."[171] And, in accordance with this teaching, we read that "the multitude of believers had but one heart and one soul."[172]

[169]John 13:35.
[170]1 John 3:10.
[171]Gal. 5:14.
[172]Acts 4:32.

And when our Lord condescended to make a new revelation of His love, He again manifested this weakness of His Heart. As St. Margaret Mary says, "One of the special effects of devotion to the Sacred Heart is to reunite divided hearts and bring peace to the soul."

∞

Learn to see Jesus in every person
Our life as Christians should be passed in seeking Jesus. St. Mary Magdalene cried out, "Tell me where thou hast laid Him, and I will take Him away."[173]

It is a faculty peculiar to intimate friends to distinguish their friends' work in anything they see; to recognize some arrangement, some painting or drawing, or some written page as an inspiration of their friends. In like manner, true faith and love find Jesus, wherever He may be. The shepherds recognized Him in His swaddling clothes; the holy women loved Him when He was bowed down by the weight of His Cross and loaded with ignominy.

The Blood of Christ has flowed over every soul that has come into this world; and when His divine Spirit

[173]John 20:15.

no longer shines therein, He Himself still shines upon them. We must look very closely and search very deeply if we sincerely wish to love our neighbor always; we must pierce through coarse envelopes and thick veils if we wish to discover what there is still left of Jesus in the soul of man; we must see "our dear neighbor in the breast of Jesus," says St. Francis de Sales. "If we do not succeed in that, we are in danger of never loving him at all."

"Let us see in every one of our neighbors, whatever his state may be, an image of Jesus Christ, and serve each one in our Lord, and our Lord in each one," St. Vincent de Paul[174] says.

"Let us consider God in His creatures — Jesus Christ in the souls of men, and their souls in God," Cardinal Bérulle[175] says. "And let us treat these souls as part of the spiritual and Mystical Body of Jesus Christ upon earth. Let us treat them reverently and carefully, as something holy and sacred."

[174]St. Vincent de Paul (c. 1580-1660), founder of the Lazarist Fathers and the Sisters of Charity.

[175]Pierre de Bérulle (1575-1629), cardinal, statesman, and theologian.

Our Lord indeed said this: "As long as you did it to one of these my least brethren, you did it to me."[176] In those souls who love the Savior dearly, there remains a habitual feeling, or at least a constant remembrance of His holy presence; they recognize Him everywhere and in everyone. However difficult charity may seem to them, however great their natural antipathy may be, however unworthy a person may appear, these souls go straight to the Savior, and kindness becomes natural to them; their patience is the exercise of love.

Mother Marie de Sales Chappuis, a pious soul whose position and duties exposed her to continual interruptions, gave a smiling and amiable welcome to all, in these simple words: "My Beloved can never disturb me." And if sometimes a first natural feeling of annoyance escaped her, as is the case with all of us — a sharp word or a cold answer — she recollected herself at once, as the vision of her Lord came before her, and said, "Pardon me, my Savior; I forgot that it was Thou."

Pious persons are often obliged to live in surroundings in which their tastes are misunderstood or opposed; they have to deal with people who are either unsympathetic

[176]Matt. 25:40.

or very trying. There are incessant interruptions, jars, and annoyances. How hard it is to be always gentle and kind! How many obstacles in the way of patience and peace! The only resource of these souls is to find Jesus everywhere, to look beyond ordinary appearances, and treat persons and things as if they were so many consecrated Hosts containing this Beloved of their souls — coming from Him, and belonging to Him.

These exalted views of creatures will also prevent weakness of heart, for they lead us at last "to love no created thing or earthly object for itself, but solely for the sake of the Creator of all things," as St. Ignatius says. "We shall be united in glory, as on earth we have been united in charity," Bossuet explains. "Let us, then, serve our brothers in the same spirit, with esteem and tenderness, and honor Jesus Christ in them."

∾

Affections
O Lord Jesus Christ, grant that we
may all be of one heart and one soul.
Then we shall all be full of kindness and
sweetness toward our neighbors, for we shall
behold their souls within the Heart of our Savior.

There, who will not love his neighbor?
Who will not bear with his imperfections?
Who will find him ungracious or wearisome?
O my Lord Jesus Christ, grant that we may be
all of one heart and one soul.

St. Francis de Sales

∞

Examination of Conscience
✦ *How is it with me in the matters of*
charity and consideration for others?

✦ *What about my thoughts? Do I give way to*
rash judgments and unjust suspicions?
Or am I ready to excuse others?

✦ *What about my feelings?*
Am I kind, anxious to please, and forgetful
of self where others are concerned?

✦ *What about my words?*
Am I always charitable and gentle?

✦ *What about my actions?*
Do I try to see Jesus in my neighbor?
Do I give him my time, charitable gifts,
and personal assistance,
as far as obedience and duty allow?

See Jesus in your neighbor

*❖ Do I always have perfect charity
toward those in authority over me and
toward any other persons with whom
I am brought into contact?*

∞

Resolution

∞

Spiritual Bouquet
*"Let us speak no more of our neighbor
except to speak well of him,
or for his benefit."*

St. Jane Frances de Chantal

Step Nineteen

∞

Listen to Christ in the Gospel

Jesus said to the chief of His Apostles, "Simon, son of John, lovest thou me? Lovest thou me more than these?"[177] It was easy for St. Peter to reply. His Lord was there, before his eyes, so good, so tender, with that radiance from His divine nature which captivated all those whom He wished to convert or confirm. The question contained the grace necessary for the answer.

Are we less happy at the distance of two thousand years from that blessed time? "No," says St. Augustine, "for the sacred words which then fell from His divine lips have been written and preserved for us. Let us listen to the words of the Gospel, as if our Lord were still in the midst of us." And let us consider that it is necessary for us to read the Gospel and to understand it.

[177]Cf. John 21:15.

∞

Christ speaks to you in the Gospel

The Gospel is the account of the words and actions of
the Word made flesh. It is therefore the mirror of Christian perfection, to which we must all go to contemplate
the image of the Holy One of God, so that by degrees
we may be remade in His likeness. Toward the end of
his life, St. Philip Neri[178] read nothing but the Gospels,
and at last only the Gospel of St. John — the Gospel
that speaks most beautifully of the love of Jesus for us
and entreats us more earnestly to become the friends
of our Savior.

"There is but one Master, who spoke to His own
and still speaks to them, in His Gospel," we hear from
Bossuet. The Lord Jesus is indeed the Word of God. "He
is the mouth of the Father, and it is He who speaks in
the Gospels," says St. Ambrose, and St. Augustine tells
us, "By means of His Gospel, Jesus, who is in Heaven,
continues to speak to us on earth."

The pages of the Gospel are like the bright star in
the East, which God sent to guide His chosen ones to

[178]St. Philip Neri (1515-1595), Italian priest who
founded the Congregation of the Oratory.

the feet of the infant Jesus. The Gospel is a kind of sacrament that conceals our Lord; and St. Augustine does not hesitate to say, "He who despises but one of these sacred words is as guilty as if he carelessly allowed a particle of the Holy Eucharist to fall to the ground."

The deeper we penetrate into the truths of the Gospel, the more fully do we find Jesus Christ. He is there, in very deed, with all His holiness and goodness, His mercy and tender love. He is the Jesus of the manger, the Jesus of Nazareth, the Jesus of the Magdalene and Zaccheus,[179] the Jesus of St. John, the Jesus of the Last Supper and of Calvary, the Jesus of the tabernacle and of my heart.

The Gospel was written for everyone — for the Carmelite nun, as well as for the woman in the world; for the saint on fire with the love of God, as well as for the poor sinner who is beginning to return to his Father from the "far-off country."[180]

"The Gospel is another way in which Jesus has chosen to dwell among us," St. Augustine says. With what respect was the book of the Gospels treated by the first Christians! They read it and meditated upon it

[179]Luke 19:2 ff.
[180]Cf. Luke 15:13.

constantly, and this custom of theirs, united to their frequent Communions, soon had the effect of bathing their souls deeply in Jesus Christ. They carried copies of the Gospel on their person; they hung them around the necks of their children, and St. Cecilia said to her judges, "I bear Him always upon my heart."

At the present day, there are many Christians who scarcely ever read the Gospel; the greater part of them know nothing of Holy Scripture, except the small portions read in the church during Mass on Sundays. Many good people, who think themselves pious, go frequently to Holy Communion, and yet die without ever having read the whole of the Gospels. Is it, then, anything to be astonished at, that characters should be so weak; that piety should be so half-hearted, misunderstood, and little practiced; and that the Heart of our dear Master should be so little known and so little understood?

∞

There are three ways to
understand the Gospel

Three dispositions are necessary to the soul who reads and wishes to understand the Gospel: prayer, meditation, and practice. "Let prayer often interrupt your spiritual reading," says St. Bonaventure. The Gospel should be read, figuratively speaking, on our knees — that is to say, in the interior and exterior dispositions of a soul who seeks and finds Jesus, under the outer shell of the written page — just as the angels announced His birth, and the shepherds recognized their Lord when they found Him "wrapped in swaddling clothes and laid in a manger."[181]

It is necessary that our good Master should explain His words to us and help us to enter into communion with Him. Without His grace and assistance, our reading will be nothing more than a study, and St. Ignatius tells us that "it is not the abundance of knowledge which fills and satisfies our souls, but the comprehension and interior love of the truths meditated upon." "No one knoweth the Father but the Son, and he to whom it shall please the Son to reveal Him."[182]

The Wise Men from the East would never have known the birth of the Infant-God, nor have found the road to Him, if they had not fixed their eyes on the miraculous star that appeared in the heavens. Thus, says

[181]Luke 2:12.
[182]Matt. 11:27.

St. Bonaventure, "every time we discover new lights and gather new meanings from the mysterious depths of the Sacred Narrative, it is as if a new messenger from Heaven were sent to our souls."

With prayer, we must use meditation; meditation will teach us to listen, "not for the voice that is heard from without, but for the inner voice of Truth, which speaks in the depths of our souls."[183]

The bee and the wasp suck the same flowers, but they do not both know how to find honey there. The wasp dips into the flowers and devours greedily. The bee gathers, prepares, and transforms the precious liquid; and when the honey is made, it is the result of the bees' intelligence and care.

In the Gospel, there is scarcely one word that has not created a saint or produced a special sanctity. Thus, St. Francis of Assisi was torn from the world by the words: "Go, sell what thou hast, and give to the poor; and come, follow me."[184] St. Francis Xavier[185] was called to

[183] *Imitation of Christ,* Bk. 3, ch. 1, no. 1.

[184] Matt. 19:21.

[185] St. Francis Xavier (1506-1552), Jesuit missionary known as the Apostle of the Indies.

the labors of the apostolate by the words: "What doth it profit a man if he shall gain the whole world and suffer the loss of his own soul?"[186]

We must all clearly understand which of all these sayings is intended for us, and hear it so distinctly that we may obey it in all its requirements. Moreover, so that we may not be mistaken, or wander off into erroneous and deluding interpretations, we must question the Church and listen to her teaching; it is her duty to guard the sacred text and to explain the truths contained therein.

Finally, the practice of our daily lives must be in accordance with the Gospel's teaching. "Always read with the intention of applying the lessons you learn to your own duties, and the faults that must be corrected in order to please God," says Fénelon. A light thrown on the will of God calls for an immediate effort; the effort we make merits for us a new light: such is the economy of grace.

The life of the saints is simply the Gospel in action. So it was that the pure little child-martyr St. Agnes and the angelic St. Aloysius[187] must have listened to the

[186]Matt. 16:26.

[187]St. Agnes, virgin and martyr; St. Aloysius Gonzaga (1568-1591), patron saint of youth.

words of Jesus: "Blessed are the clean of heart."[188] So it was that St. Francis of Assisi comprehended all that was included in those other words: "Blessed are the poor in spirit,"[189] and that St. Francis de Sales made his own another beatitude: "Blessed are the meek."[190] As Bossuet says, "To enjoy the words of Jesus Christ is a proof that we enjoy Him, and the best preparation for enjoying Him forever in Heaven."

Perhaps we ourselves are afraid of evangelical austerity. We are afraid of anything that restrains us. We fear sacrifices and suffering. We are waiting to give up all until the hour comes when we shall have nothing to give. Then we shall never have comprehended the Gospel, or the words of God, or our good Savior. If it is so with us, how can we ever expect to enjoy His friendship? Are we not afraid of being "one day condemned for having listened to His words without obeying them, for having known Him without loving Him, and for believing in Him without keeping His commandments"?[191]

[188]Matt. 5:8.
[189]Matt. 5:3
[190]Matt. 5:4.
[191]Cf. *Imitation of Christ*, Bk. 3, ch. 2, no. 3.

"Let us therefore read," says Bossuet, "but let us read with our hearts, and not merely with our eyes; let us profit by all we hear, and adore all that we do not understand."

∞

Affections

O my sweet Teacher, every one of Thy
words is for us a living source, a feast, a sun!
We have gleaned them partly from Thy Holy Gospel:
how can we thank Thee enough for having condescended
to allow them to be preserved there? And I am also certain
that it is because Thy words can do us so much good
that Thou didst love to speak to us so sweetly.

Mercifully help us, beloved Master,
to profit by Thy holy teaching.

∞

Examination of Conscience

* *Do I read every day some verses of the Holy Gospel?*
Do I pray and meditate while reading,
so that I may have a clearer
knowledge of my divine Lord?

* *Do I use a commentary, so that I may*
understand the Gospel more perfectly?

⁜ *Am I ready to follow the spirit of Jesus in all its austerity, in all its requirements, and in everything that pertains to my state of life?*

∞

Resolution

∞

Spiritual Bouquet
"You will be saints in body and soul if the words of the Gospel are continually upon your lips and within your hearts."

St. John Chrysostom

Step Twenty

∞

Turn to Jesus for direction

"Jesus is the faithful Friend," says St. Francis de Sales. "He will guide you, govern you, and take care of you. Ask Him to teach you whatever you ought to do; do nothing without His advice." Let us, then, first ask for the advice of our Savior, and, second, let us listen to and follow the advice He gives us.

∞

You should consult Jesus in everything

The saints called our Lord's advice "the light of life." It is as difficult for us to be our own guide in the life of the soul — and often also in temporal difficulties — as for a blind man to walk alone, without anyone to help him and see for him.

We can find many advisers among our fellowmen, especially in the priest who stands in the place of Jesus for us, and to whom the divine Counselor wishes us to have recourse, so that we may be protected against possibly grave delusions. But the best of all advisers, the first of all, is our dear Lord. Isaiah prophesied that "His name should be called Counselor";[192] and our Lord Himself said to His Apostles, "You call me Master and Lord, and you say well, for so I am."[193]

He is not only learned and all-seeing; He is indeed "the Light, the True Light, which enlightened every man that cometh into the world . . . full of grace and truth."[194] When the sun does not shine, we require artificial light to know the valleys and walk in their paths; but when this King of stars shines, every other light grows pale and is useless to us. Thus St. John says of the beatified soul, that it "has no need of the sun, nor of the moon [i.e., of any created light], for the glory of God hath enlightened it, and the Lamb is the lamp thereof."[195]

This Lamb is my own Christ Jesus, who has chosen me for His own and has promised henceforth to be my

[192] Isa. 9:6.
[193] John 13:13.
[194] John 1:9, 14.
[195] Apoc. 21:23 (RSV = Rev. 21:23).

Counselor and Light. Therefore, I ought to consult Him often before consulting any other person — before taking any action. He gave us an example of this. He said, "I cannot of myself do anything. As I hear, so I judge; and my judgment is just, because I seek not my own will, but the will of Him that sent me."[196] He is a loving Son, obedient to His Father and dependent upon Him.

"When anyone asks your advice," said St. Jane Frances de Chantal, "do not answer until you have entered into yourself, to ask God to inspire you with an answer." Perhaps you have consulted some holy religious, or priest, or some really pious person. And while you are speaking to them, these holy souls become recollected, and seem to be listening for some voice speaking within them. They do not trust their own wisdom, so they ask the advice of Jesus before they speak; they listen to the Lord, who speaks within them, and ask counsel of light at its deepest source.

Being also enlightened by the doctrine of the Church, they judge according to what they hear, and it is this dependence on the Holy Spirit, united to divinely authorized teaching, that gives so much authority and unction

[196]John 5:30.

to the words of the saints; their secret persuasiveness draws us to them and, through them, to God. St. Augustine tells us, "To be able to speak to others the words of God, we must have listened to them in our own soul."

If we wish to live with Jesus as His friends, we must ask His advice as often as possible. By degrees we shall make Jesus so much our friend that we shall never wish to do anything without asking His permission — without begging Him to tell us if it will be for His glory and pleasing to Him.

Let us always consult Him. In all difficulties, in all doubts, and even with regard to our daily occupations, we shall gain much if we ask our Lord to be with us and if we think how He would have acted. When we draw near our Savior, we receive light from Him; and on every occasion when we thus draw near to Him, our recollected soul is bathed, in that divine communion, in the necessary strength to fulfill all its duties perfectly.

∞

Silence and courage allow you
to hear and heed Jesus' advice

Two conditions are necessary for hearing the voice of Jesus and understanding His advice: silence in listening and courage in obeying. From the admirable rules St. Ignatius has given on the discerning of spirits, we learn that the evil spirit speaks loudly, cries out, makes a great deal of noise; he is not "well bred." On the contrary, the good Spirit, who is the Holy Spirit, is always gentle and peaceful; He speaks very low — like "a whistling of a gentle air"[197] — and is heard only as a breeze of evening. "What silence we must keep if we do not wish to lose one of His words!" exclaims Bossuet. "So true is this," says Père Tissot, "that when two voices are heard within us, if we wish to know to which we ought to listen, we must remember that the low and gentle voice is the good voice."

For example: you receive a letter that is not very civil; someone foolishly repeats to you an unkind speech made about you; the friend upon whom you relied most forgets you or betrays your confidence: one of those little nothings happens which causes a tempest of rage in persons who are very excitable, who have not much virtue, and are not really united to Jesus. Immediately you fall into a great state of excitement; the emotion rushes from your heart to your lips if you are unmortified, if you do

---

[197] 3 Kings 19:12 (RSV = 1 Kings 19:12).

not pause to reflect. Remember: It is the evil angel who is passing by; he is stirring up your soul, noisily, and furiously, "as water falling upon stone," says St. Ignatius.

And while this terrible storm is breaking over you, another voice within the depths of your soul — gentle as the voice of Jesus, calm as eternity — says to you quite simply, "If only you will wait a little; if only you will discuss this affair with me, if only you will learn from Jesus, who is so humble, so patient, so merciful, what to think, what to say, and what to do." This is the voice of your good angel, touching your soul lightly and gently, "as a drop of water penetrating a sponge."

This is the voice of Truth. And those souls who listen to it know how to observe the silence that unites us to God, isolates us from outside agitations, and separates us from the worthless part of ourselves, for that which often causes the most commotion is self and self-love.

"Be, therefore, recollected and interior," Bossuet recommends, "for the Doctor of our souls speaks within us. Where are you running to when you fly from one distraction to another, from one visit to another, from one trouble to another? You are rushing away from your better self, and at the same time from the Holy Spirit, who wishes to speak to you."

When the voice of God is heard, we must have the courage to obey it. The young man in the Gospel asked our Savior's advice and heard His answer, but "he went away sad, for he had great possessions."[198]

And St. James says, "Be ye doers of the word, and not hearers only, deceiving your own selves."[199] How many times our duty appears so clear, the will of God is so plainly to be seen, but an effort, a sacrifice, some trouble, is necessary. How ingenious we are then in deceiving ourselves, persuading ourselves that God cannot be so exacting, and concluding that we will put off taking any action until later on! Then the light grows dim, our attraction toward renunciation and perfection is blunted, and the love of God in our souls grows weaker and weaker. This, alas, is the history of many souls, who always remain half-hearted, miserable, and discouraged.

On the other hand, what complete assurance is given by the constant practice of consulting our Lord on every occasion and following His advice, before beginning a friendship or forming any ties, before paying a visit, or before making a confidence! What an efficacious

[198]Matt. 19:22.
[199]James 1:22.

remedy it presents against every rebellion or surprise of nature! If we always consulted our Savior before giving an order or a counsel, before making an observation, or uttering a complaint or criticism, before asking a permission or a change of employment — if every evening, before our crucifix, we went over all the events of the day and asked the advice of Jesus on everything we had heard, seen, desired, loved, or said during that day, what a help it would be to us in keeping up the perfection of our spiritual life!

∞

Affections

My divine Savior,
I wish absolutely only for that
which is Thy will for me, and I would
indeed be happy if I could always know Thy will.
My whole desire is never to stray from Thy holy will;
all my fear is lest I should deceive myself in this matter.
Thou hast made me realize that it is Thy wish that I
should always have Thee present before my eyes,
so that I may say nothing and do nothing without
consulting Thee. My only wish is to obey
Thee, O my Divine Master.

The Foundress of the Sisters of Maria Teresa

∞

Examination of Conscience
• *Do I ask the advice of our Lord in everything?*
Do I really believe that no detail of my life is too insignificant
for Him to be interested in it? If I had consulted Him before taking
a certain step or performing a certain action — in consequence of
which I am now suffering — would I be a prey to these regrets?

• *In what should I chiefly consult Him today?*

• *If I complain that I cannot hear His voice,*
does not that proceed from my want of recollection?
Have I stifled His voice within my soul when
He has asked me for some sacrifice?

∞
Resolution

∞
Spiritual Bouquet
"Listen to the good Master
who dwells within your soul;
do nothing without consulting Him;
do everything as in His sight."

Jacques Bossuet

Step Twenty-One

∞

Rest in Jesus

Human nature presents this strange contradiction: incessant longing for rest and perpetual restlessness. This is really on account of two simultaneous reflections: on the happiness that we anticipate and on the labor necessary for gaining it.

Our labor would be nonetheless active and fruitful if we performed it, as St. Francis de Sales tells us, "by allowing ourselves to be carried by our divine Lord, as a little child is carried in the arms of his mother. Our Lord has a continual care for His children, making them walk before Him, holding them by the hand when passing over difficult places, and often carrying them Himself."

Therefore, let us consider that we must first lean upon the arm of our Savior and then we must allow Him to carry us.

∞

You must rely on Jesus

"If we wish to depend entirely upon our loving Savior, and to be in real union with Him," says Père Tissot, "it is not enough to ask His advice; we must also lean upon His arm. A husband invites his wife to accompany him. What does she do? She takes his arm. She can quite well walk alone; there is no great difficulty in taking a few steps. But because she loves her husband so much, because she wishes to depend upon him entirely, it is a joy, a real pleasure, to lean upon him; so she takes his arm."

To take the arm of our Lord? It is divine Wisdom that has said, in the words of the bride in the Canticle of Canticles, "Put me as a seal upon thy heart, as a seal upon thy arm: for love is strong as death."[200] It is a disgrace that souls, after two thousand years of Christianity, should be astonished at such a thought as this. Long before the Incarnation revealed to us the love of our Emmanuel, long before we knew anything of His Words, or His tenderness, or His Eucharist, David cried out, "Though I should walk in the midst of the shadow of

[200]Cant. 8:6 (RSV = Song of Sol. 8:6).

death, I will fear no evils, for Thou art with me; Thy rod and Thy staff, they have comforted me."[201]

This divine Master is still more the "strength and comfort" of the saints of the New Testament. St. Rose of Lima was naturally extremely timid; her mother was also very easily frightened. On one occasion, St. Rose was in a dwelling separated from her own house by a long garden. Night came on, and darkness fell upon her, terror seized her, and she dared not cross the garden. She called her mother, and her mother called upon her husband. Then, leaning upon his arm, she went to meet her child. When Rose heard her mother speaking so cheerfully, she exclaimed, "How is this? It is quite sufficient for my mother to lean upon the arm of a man to have no more fear; and I, who can lean upon the arm of my divine Beloved, I am afraid!" Henceforth Rose of Lima never knew fear.

Our Lord owes us the help of His arm whenever we perform any work proper to our vocation or fulfill any of our duties. We need only ask Him for this assistance. Interior souls call upon Him in their most ordinary occupations. "When it is my turn to sweep the corridors,"

[201] Ps. 22:4 (RSV = Ps. 23:4).

said a religious accustomed to great simplicity with her Lord, "I always take our Lord with me. I lean upon His arm and think that He is doing the work along with me. Then I say to myself, 'Well done! Now, when my Sisters pass this place, they will inhale the good odor of Jesus.'"

This is real union. How many souls there are who, in the midst of sorrows, sufferings, and temptations, are comforted and strengthened by such thoughts as these! "It is Jesus who gives them this increase of faith, hope, and charity, who bestows on them these interior joys which call and draw the soul to heavenly things and the care of their salvation, giving them confidence and peace in their Creator and their Lord," says St. Ignatius. It would be good for us always to turn thus to our best Friend whenever we are in difficulties, or are suffering from annoyance or deception coming from other friends.

How far from such delicate and noble ideas as these are the spiteful feelings, the bitterness and rebellious murmurs, that often attend our disappointments and failures or the mere forgetfulness of those who ought to remember us. Jesus says to everyone, as He said to St. Mechtildis, "I will be to thee a most faithful friend; thou shalt lean upon me, and I will always come to Thine assistance."

∞

You must allow Christ to carry you

St. Margaret Mary gave this advice: "Be always abandoned and sacrificed to the Heart of Jesus, keeping your souls in peace. He will never forsake you, but will take special care of you in proportion as you trust in Him." It is a great thing to abandon ourselves entirely and lean upon the arm of our Lord.

A still more touching proof of our love and trust is to allow ourselves to be carried. St. Augustine says, "It is not a question of idle repose, but of perfectly calm activity and labor," for real love is not satisfied with uniting itself to Jesus by faith and the tenderness of love, or with sleeping and doing nothing in mistaken tranquillity; it will add to all this a courageous and constant imitation of the virtues of the divine Master.

"We must not only allow ourselves to be drawn," says Bossuet. "We must use all our strength and run after Him." When we have labored courageously at any good work, as if everything depended upon us, we must wait calmly and patiently for Him upon whom everything depends, for the success of our labor.

Under the ancient law, God had already said, "I will carry you," not only during infancy, or when you begin to take your first steps, but "even to your old age and to your gray hairs." "I will carry you, and I will be your Savior and Deliverer."[202]

Under the new law — the law of love — and with regard to His friends, our Lord made other promises. Since then, He has shown Himself to us as the Good Shepherd, carrying the lost and wounded sheep upon His shoulders. He is indeed the bearer of our souls.

So, whether we will or not, we are carried in the arms of the Word made flesh. St. Paul says that God "upholds all things, by the word of His power."[203]

It is quite a different thing to be carried, and to allow oneself willingly to be carried. You see two women passing by, each of them carrying her child. One of the children is in a great state of agitation. He struggles, and seems only to be happy away from his mother. He looks in front; he looks behind; he turns this way and that way, fighting and kicking. He is not still for a moment. The poor mother can scarcely hold him; he will not be carried. The other child, on the contrary, rests quietly upon his mother's breast, as if he were asleep. From time to

[202]Cf. Isa. 46:3-4.
[203]Heb. 1:3.

time, however, his pure and gentle eyes open widely, and he fixes them upon his one "polestar": his mother's face. He smiles at her and then sleeps again; his little soul rests in a peace that nothing can trouble. He allows himself to be carried. "It matters nothing to him whether his mother walks through green meadows, or on a path bordered by precipices," says St. Francis de Sales. "It matters not if she carries him on her right arm or on her left."

Our Lord wishes to carry us in His loving arms, and we struggle and will not rest there. St. John of the Cross says, "We act exactly as little children, when their mothers wish to carry them, to save them from the fatigue of walking. They scream and cry, and finally slide out of their mothers' arms onto the ground. But, after all, they cannot walk, and they only prevent their mothers from advancing." We look behind and look before; we try to escape from the loving arms of our divine Lord, and we injure ourselves in so doing; we will not allow Him to carry us.

How many forms does our resistance to His Holy Spirit take! He knows how to draw good from past evil. He knows so well how to open the path of holiness to us in the present. His gentle kindness carefully prepares for us everything necessary for our perfection in the future.

Our Lord said once to a very holy soul, "Sleep upon my Heart; I will rest in thine." And it seemed to her also as if He commanded invisible powers and said these other words: "Awake not my Beloved till she please."[204]

Our Lord repays a hundredfold anyone who loves Him and wishes to be His friend.[205] "Grace is given in sufficient measure to him who leans upon the support of his Creator and his Lord," says St. Ignatius. Therefore, when we rest in our Savior's arms, or labor with Him in the rough paths of sacrifice and self-abnegation, we shall always be at peace; we shall increase in courage for the performance of all good works; we shall deserve to be carried by Him. And when at last we sleep in His arms, we shall enter upon our eternal rest in Heaven.

∞

Affections
Come to my assistance, O Lord.
Thou art my God; Thou art my Father.

[204]Cant. 3:5 (RSV = Song of Sol. 3:5).
[205]Cf. Matt. 19:29.

Let Thy strong right hand
uphold Thy poor servant.

O my poor soul, be always dependent
upon thy divine Bridegroom.

O Jesus, I desire never to be separated from
Thy gentle hand, which leads and carries me
in the way of Thy holy will. May Thy left
hand be under my head, O my Savior, and
may Thy right hand embrace me.

St. Jane Frances de Chantal

∞

Examination of Conscience

* *Do I constantly lean upon the arm of our Lord?*
  If I do not, why is it? Is it because I am not
  recollected enough, not courageous enough?

* *Does the thought that Jesus is there strengthen me*
  in times of trouble and temptation? Does it
  restrain me from small faults and imperfections?

* *Do I allow Jesus to carry me — being and doing all that He*
wishes, as He wishes, and when He wishes; laboring with courage,
and resting in peace, when I have confided myself and all to Him?

* *In what way am I going to practice*
what I have just learned in this meditation?

A Pocket Retreat for Catholics

∞
Resolution

∞
Spiritual Bouquet
*"O Mary, grant that Jesus may
always rest in my heart, and that I may
always rest in the Heart of Jesus."*

St. Alphonsus Liguori

Step Twenty-Two

∞

Abandon yourself to God's will

St. Francis de Sales says that all the things of this world are only puerilities. "When we reach the evening of life, we despise earthly things, as we do the little houses of wood and mud which, in our childhood, we took so much trouble to build, and which cost us so many tears when they were destroyed. We shall be quite safe when we reach the house of our heavenly Father." He has taught us to value nothing but God, His holy will, and His service.

"Every creature should become for us a mirror of life, and a book of holiness,"[206] to guide us in the way to union with Him — first, by showing us that Jesus is present in every event of our lives and, second, by teaching us how to find Jesus in all that happens to us.

[206] *Imitation of Christ*, Bk. 2, ch. 4, no. 1.

∞

Jesus is present in every event of your life

There is often, even in souls who think themselves very pious, a kind of practical atheism. We see God in the tabernacle, but we do not see Him in the world, in society, or in the human heart. We do not see Him everywhere, yet "God is the Lord who hath made all things."[207] "I form the light and create darkness; I make peace and create evil: I the Lord that do all these things."[208]

No created thing can act if God does not ordain or permit it. Reason discloses this truth to us, and faith only confirms it. "God our Lord is present in all His creatures, by essence, presence, and power," says St. Ignatius.

We are willing that it should be so, when we speak to Him, or meditate upon Him, and when it is a question of God alone. But in the practice of our daily life, we are less consistent. When God comes to us under the veil of a created will, or in the cloud of earthly events, our hearts are troubled, our minds are disturbed, and we can no longer see the Providence of our good God in these humiliations, deceptions, untoward events,

[207]Cf. Isa. 44:24.
[208]Isa. 45:7.

small evils, and the nothings which we call our *crosses*, and which are our habitual trials.

Yet it is not only God who is in all these things; it is the *good* God, "acting and working for me in all these created things," as St. Ignatius says. Everything that God wills, by commandment or by permission, as a prohibition or a punishment, is always the divine power influencing every creature for its own good — everyone according to his fashion, his measure, and his rank. Observe the words of St. Paul: "This is the will of God, your sanctification."[209]

Let us remember that our Savior lived on earth for every one of us and that He still continues His most holy life in the humble little lives of us all. It is thus that He wills and accomplishes the will of His Father with regard to me. He has said *yes* for me to everything that His Father will require of me; the will of God with regard to me has been transmitted to me by my Jesus — even if I am to be ill today, or contradicted, or tempted, or in difficulties, failures, and every kind of trial. Each event of my life comes to me as if it were impregnated with the filial obedience of my Savior. Henceforth,

[209] 1 Thess. 4:3.

there is only one attitude fitting for me: to abandon myself, to renounce myself, to give myself up, as Jesus in His Passion, as Jesus in the Eucharist.

How good it would be for us if we could accept everything that happens as a means of glorifying God and leading us to love Him more! A little bird knows so well how to crack the seed that is given to it, how to refuse and reject the shell and swallow the grain. As for us, during most of our time, we do just the contrary: we attach ourselves so much to the outer envelope that we lose the fruit.

"Now I will show you the great answer to the enigma of life, the target of perfection, at which we must all take aim: to find out what God wishes, to do it cheerfully, or at least courageously, and to love this will of God," says St. Francis de Sales. "The loving Heart of our Redeemer arranges all the events of their lives to the advantage of those souls who give themselves up to His love without any reserve."

∞

You can discover Jesus all around you
"Our Lord," said a pious soul, "gives Himself in continual communion to the soul who is perfectly united to

His divine will. He loves that soul to receive Him, not only every morning at the altar, but every instant of the day, by means of his little joys and sorrows, and his association with his neighbor, who gives God to us, and to whom we give Him."

At the commencement of Lent, a superior of the Visitation Order, a soul closely united to her Lord, proposed this challenge to her nuns: "Let us take everything as coming from the hand of our loving God and Savior. We will see Him everywhere. We will receive Him continually. Everything that happens shall be to us as accidents or species under which He hides Himself. Everything shall be to us a mystery of love, the sacrament of the moment that is passing, a communion that never ceases, a feast that has no evening. Created things shall disappear for us, and shadows shall flee away. We will see everything in the clear light of the day of our free life. We will taste the abundant sweetness of divine Love." This is indeed to see the Creator in His creation, and the Lord of all things in the things He has made.

"Faith is a bright ray from Heaven," says St. Francis de Sales, "which makes us see God in all things, and everything in God." St. Jane Frances de Chantal tells us, "The grace above all other graces is to be submissive to His holy will in all things."

When we have thus comprehended our divine Savior and learned to work with Him — each one according to his or her vocation — everything will appear to us equally good. "Whether we are nothing, or of much consequence or of little," says St. Jane Frances de Chantal, "whether we command or obey; whether we obey this person or that; if we are humiliated or forgotten; if we are in need or well provided for; if we have leisure or are overloaded with work; if we are alone or with companions whom we love; if our way is plain before our eyes or if we cannot see it at all, and know not where to place our feet; if we are in consolation or desolate and dry, and even tempted in our darkness; if we are well or ill, or on a sickbed for years; if we are to live long, or die soon, or die at once — all is accepted willingly. If others receive more graces than we, let us rejoice in it, for the sake of God; the degree of glory to which we aspire is just so much as God thinks fit to give us. Our whole life is simply a living *yes* to God, an *amen*, which will one day be united to the eternal *amen* of Heaven."

It is the desire of Jesus to give Himself, and events are only the means by which His love places Him within our reach. Left alone, our faith is too weak, our self-love too little realized, and our trust too limited. To give pleasure to God by a holy life must be sufficient for us, until we can give back to Him that which He Himself has given us.

St. Teresa says, "He takes care of me in everything. My only thought is how to please Him"; and St. Ignatius says, "When a soul is thus disposed with regard to every event of life, trusting in God alone, and obedient to His will in all things, desiring only to be ruled and governed by his Creator and Lord, that soul is then honored by becoming the property of the Divine Majesty, who takes delight in His faithful servant, filling him with consolations, and helping him to bring forth an abundance of perfect spiritual fruit, which continually increases, to the greater glory of the Divine Goodness."

∞

Affections

*Lord, Thou knowest what is best. Let this or that
be done as Thou wilt. Give what Thou wilt, how much
Thou wilt, and when Thou wilt. Do with me as Thou
knowest, and as best pleaseth Thee, and is most for Thine
honor. Put me where Thou wilt, and do with me in all things*

*according to Thy holy will. Let Thy will be mine, and let
my will always follow Thine and agree perfectly with it.*

Imitation of Christ, Bk. 3, ch. 15, no. 3

∞

Examination of Conscience
 * *Do I try to see God in every event of my life?
Is my conversation in agreement with this thought?*

 * *Do I try to control my joys and calm my sorrows by
looking steadfastly at my Savior, who sends them to me?*

 * *Am I perfectly content with my state of life, my employment,
my health, and everything else, for the sake of God?*

 * *Do I keep my soul in peace after I have confided an undertaking
to Him or recommended an affair to His guidance?*

 * *Have I decided to trust my Savior in everything?*

∞

Resolution

∞

Spiritual Bouquet
*"Yes, Lord, if Thou dost wish this, I wish it.
If Thou dost not wish it, neither do I."*

St. Francis de Sales

Step Twenty-Three

∞

Share your joys with Jesus

St. Thomas has laid down the maxim that joy is the condition and result of a real friendship. "A friend," he says, "takes his pleasure and joy in living with his friend."

This is exactly what our loving Master said once to St. Mechtildis, "Thou art my joy, and I am thine." And He also said to St. Gertrude, "I associate thee with myself in all my joys through the love that I have for thee, and I enjoy nothing if I do not enjoy it with thee."

It is a sign that we really understand our Lord when we offer Him in a childlike manner everything that has power to gladden our hearts.

Let us meditate on this practice of abandonment to our Lord — first, in our joys and, second, in our merits.

∞

Joy is a gift from God

Jansenism[210] and all the opponents of a life of union with our divine Savior have contracted the Heart of God on the side of the generosity that gives and have straitened and almost closed it on the side that receives. Forgetting that gentle and tender ways are natural to Divine Wisdom, they teach us to tremble continually in the service of God. Thus, devotion assumes that dark and gloomy form that St. Francis de Sales blames so wittily and so severely. Thus, many books of piety lay down impracticable theories and are full of such heights that an angel would scarcely be able to breathe thereon. Thus, there is a conventional idea that all sanctity is confined to the cloister, and the rest of the world is represented as an abyss of wickedness.

The result is that people despise "this maligned piety," and if a few generous souls are brave enough to climb the rugged path of devotion, "they soon come down

[210]The heresy of Jansenism denied man's free will to accept or reject God's grace and claimed that Christ did not die for all, that man cannot keep all the commandments, and that only the most worthy should receive Communion.

from the mountain, irritated and discouraged, like a man who has wandered into the bushes and broken his knees against the rocks," as Fr. Faber[211] says.

St. Basil calls the Devil "the Angel of Melancholy," and certainly "that evil spirit delights in sadness, because he is sad and melancholy himself and will be so for all eternity. Therefore, he wishes everyone to be like him," says St. Francis de Sales. Do you really wish to be purified from your sins, and to go on from good to better in the service of God? If so, meditate upon the following words of St. Ignatius: "It is the special characteristic of God and His angels, when they act within a soul, to fill it with real happiness and true spiritual joy. On the contrary, the special characteristic of the enemy is to fight against this joy."

Joy is one of the fruits of the Holy Spirit.[212] It comes after love, because it is the radiation of love. We may say that it is the *smile* of love. St. Thomas tells us, "To rejoice is a duty mixed up with the duty of loving. Joy is the fruit of love, satisfied with the presence and

[211]Frederick William Faber (1814-1863), Oratorian and hymn writer.
[212]Gal. 5:22.

possession of the beloved one or with a clear realization of its own happiness." When we seek joy, we seek God. When we are joyful, we are rendering Him justice, for we are publishing the truth that "His yoke is sweet, and His burden light,"[213] and that no happiness can be compared to the happiness of those who serve Him.

What care St. Francis de Sales took to make piety amiable and joyous, because, as he said, we can repulse the Devil without repulsing all the good things that he tries to corrupt! He says, "Always walk cheerfully along the road to Heaven. Keep your heart and soul in the spirit of a holy joy — a gracious, charitable, and well-regulated joy. If anyone is kind and affectionate to you, think that it is all the will of God, and thank Him for this little consolation."

There is always this way of sanctifying our joy: to see Jesus within our souls and accept Him in all that He sends us.

St. Mary Magdalene de' Pazzi ran into the convent garden, picked a flower, and inhaled its perfume. Immediately her soul rose far above all earthly joys, and she cried out, "How good Thou art, my Jesus! From all

[213]Cf. Matt. 11:30.

eternity, Thou hast destined this flower to rejoice the heart of a poor sinner such as I am."

St. Gertrude, wasted with fever, saw a bunch of grapes and asked for it in all simplicity to quench the thirst of Jesus, who suffered within her.

Our joys would be doubled, and all our happiness sanctified, if we took care to share them all with our Savior. Our little triumphs of success, far from nourishing pride or inclining us to it, should always throw us into the Heart of our good Master. Moreover, our very sorrows should become, as Bossuet says, "joys in the Cross, as those of Jesus were."

∞

You should rejoice humbly in your merits

Our merits are, indeed, the joys of the soul — true joys in our Lord. To be holy, to be crowned with great merit, also gives Jesus the joy He prefers to all others. In Heaven, the Heart of the God-Man continues to share in the joy of His friends. He is as happy on that account as when He was caressed by His Virgin Mother, when St. John gave Him the love of his virgin heart, or when He received the purified devotion of the Magdalene. The smallest act of virtue attracts His attention, brings His Heart nearer to mine, and makes me more entirely His.

Therefore, I ought carefully to guard all these treasures for His sake; yet I am allowed to find therein my sweetest enjoyment in my life of exile. God sees Himself as He is, and that vision is His joy. "All the merits of the saints," says St. Augustine, "are gifts of God. If a faithful servant of His says, 'I am a saint,' it is the confession of a grateful soul. To lift our hearts to God is not to lift them up against God. If you say, 'I am a saint by my own power,' you are proud and presumptuous; if you say, 'I am not a saint,' you are ungrateful to the grace of God. Acknowledge, therefore, that you possess the gifts of God but that they do not proceed from yourself; then you will be neither proud nor ungrateful."

Nevertheless, it generally happens that holy persons see the good they are doing and forget it.

"Bees make their honey in solitude and silence," says St. Francis de Sales, "and the ordinary rule is that noise does no good and that good works are noiseless." How seldom is this the practice of certain devout souls, who occupy themselves with good works! Silence is the one thing to which they resign themselves with difficulty; they take so much pleasure in thinking and speaking of themselves! An old writer says that they are like grass-hoppers, chirping continually and living in idleness. Another compares them to a hen, who, as soon as she has laid an egg, cackles so loudly that she calls for the hand that takes it away from her. There is nothing, or almost nothing, of our Lord in their conversation, and the expressions of humility that they use on such occasions are only artifices to increase the food of their self-love.

Finally, the true friend of Jesus, certain of His love, and knowing that He rewards us far above our merits or our desires, labors patiently in the work of his salvation and of the divine glory, keeping his soul in peace. He trusts so entirely in his Beloved that he does not waste time in counting up his own merits or continually ask-ing to what degree of the spiritual life he has attained. The laborer, when he has sown his wheat, waits pa-tiently for the sun, rain, and dew to do their work. He does not dig up the furrows every morning to see what progress the corn is making. And the soul abandoned to God knows that He will work within him as He pleases.

St. Gertrude says, "I act as a mother acts toward her little child. If she cannot adorn him with gold and sil-ver, because he could not support the weight of them, she makes him a garland of sweet flowers." How good for us to bring all our poor little treasures to Jesus and leave our miseries to His great mercy! This is the way, St. Teresa explains, "to expand our soul in holiness and render it capable of serving God in peace, rest, and joy." It is sufficient for us to know that there is no pleasure that can equal the pleasure of really pleasing God.

∞

Affections

How good Thou art, O my Jesus!
Thou hast given me joys and successes this day and
often. I have not seen in any of them the affection of
creatures, but only the smile of Thy soul upon mine.
Whatever anyone admires and loves in me is Thy gift.

Every evening I will relate to Thee, as to my best friend,
the joys of my heart and my soul; then I will forget them
all. Thy Heart shall keep them for me, as I would
have them kept in Thy divine Heart.

The Private Journal of a Pious Soul

∞

Examination of Conscience
- *Is my piety really amiable, joyous,*
  and agreeable to everyone?

* *Do I wish for no joys, except those I can share with Jesus? When I have any pleasure, am I accustomed to carry it to Him at once?*

* *Is my soul sufficiently free from scruples to allow me to rejoice at being clever, or esteemed, or loved, provided always that I can attract others to Jesus by His own gifts to me?*

* *Am I discreet with regard to my good works?*

* *Do I labor with my whole heart for my sanctification, and do I abandon to Jesus the care of my sanctification according to the measure of His will and glory?*

∞

Resolution

∞

Spiritual Bouquet
"We must always sing as we serve God; that is to say, we must always serve Him with holy joy."

St. Augustine

Step Twenty-Four

∞

Share your sorrows with Jesus

Suffering waits upon the cradle of the infant, and the farther we advance in life, the more we see that every soul has its trials. If Faith did not speak, no human reason could explain this mystery. The Christian alone, and better still the soul united to Jesus, knows why our tears flow so often in this valley of life, and at the same time they feel the touch of a heavenly hand, which passes tenderly over their heads to support and comfort them. Every suffering is for us "the chalice which my Father hath given me to drink."[214] "It is from His love that all our sorrows as well as all our joys in this life proceed," St. Ignatius tells us.

The mission of sorrow is, first, to detach us from creatures and then to attach us to Jesus.

[214]Cf. John 18:11.

∞

Suffering detaches you from creatures

In the terrestrial Paradise, there was no suffering. What pain does now, love did then. The human heart turned to God naturally, as the river flows to the ocean, as the flower gives out its perfume. After the Fall of man, the Divine Tenderness had recourse to other means to bring the prodigal child — still loved — back to his Father's house. Here the part of suffering comes in. "Divine Love has made our lives here a medicinal and healing pain," says St. Augustine.

The first service that suffering renders us is to establish us in the truth. To have suffered greatly is to have learned, like students acquainted with many languages, to understand all and to be understood by all. We live in time so that we may become worthy of eternity — not to sit down here and dwell only with finite and created things. "We have not here a lasting city, but we seek one that is to come."[215]

Suffering puts us to the pinch, makes us stumble against walls, and covers us with blood from the stones and thorns of the road. Then, deprived of all things, we

[215]Heb. 13:14.

try to console ourselves with the companions of our exile. But sooner or later, trials, disappointments, injuries, desertion, death, and the emptiness of all created things warn us that it is God alone who never changes and whose faithfulness and love for us will never fail. "Those whom God loves with a special love of predilection," St. Ignatius says, "He takes particular care to detach from all the joys that pass away, by the sorrows and sufferings of this present life." During the whole of our life, suffering is a guiding torch, and if our eyes will only open to its light, if only our heart will resign itself, we will find that, in Dante's words, "trial remarries us to God."

Worldly persons vainly regret their youth and mourn uselessly over their vanished attractions. But God knows how to restore the beauty of souls. He purifies them by suffering and expiation, nailing them to the Cross with their Savior. "I tremble," said St. Augustine, "when I see a sinner happy."

Moreover, we have only to follow the path of suffering in any individual man at different periods of his life, and it is easy to see that an intelligent and tender hand is wounding him in the very places that have most need of purification. Such is the effect of a humiliation given to the proud, an opportunity refused to those who seek enjoyment, a state of submission imposed upon independent spirits; and always it is the gentle hand of our good God sprinkling bitterness over everything that we have loved more than Him or outside of Him.

Finally, suffering puts the crowning touch upon the sanctity of souls. This is why God often gives us joy in our early life and reserves our sorrows for our more advanced age. This is why His saints have been more tried than others and why Jesus suffered most of all. To become a thing of beauty, the block of marble needs the sculptor's hand, the diamond needs cutting; incense must be burned before it can give out its sweet perfume. Man may strive after perfection, but he scarcely has the courage to try hard enough; therefore, to help him on his way to perfection, God sends him suffering and sorrow.

"These disappointments and troubles," St. Ignatius says, "while they detach our souls from earthly things, contribute still more powerfully to acquire for us a greater degree of glory, if only we receive them with patience and gratitude, as all benefits coming from the love of a Father deserve to be received."

∞

Suffering should draw you closer to Jesus

"When God bruises us with the rod of His chastisements," says Lacordaire, "is it not that we may seek no other head than the head of our Savior; no other eyes but His eyes; no other lips but His lips; no other shoulder to rest upon but His shoulder, all bruised and torn with the whips of His scourging; no other hands and feet to kiss but His hands and feet, pierced with nails for the love of us? His design is that He should be loved by us in return, and His whole Providence is directed to this end." He Himself "suffered martyrdom that He might be loved by those who suffer."

It was when the prodigal son was hungry, when he was steeped in misery, that he remembered the joys of his father's house and arose to throw himself into the arms of that loving father. St. Francis de Sales says, "God has commanded creatures to give us no satisfaction, in order that we may be forced to return to Him. We return more often by force than from pure love; yet He is always kind and tender in His reception of us." St. Clement of Alexandria[216] tells us, "The Heart of my

[216]St. Clement of Alexandria (c. 150-c. 215), theologian.

God is like the loving breast of a mother, resting upon which, I forget all the sorrows of this life," and, says St. Gregory Nazianzen, "it is there that all my sufferings find rest."

"It is not enough to take up our cross," St. Francis de Sales tells us. "We have still to follow our Lord. If we do not follow Him, our sufferings will crucify us as they did the impenitent thief. Instead of profiting by them, we shall grow worse." When pain approaches or touches us, far from avoiding it, let us salute it as the messenger of peace. Let us kiss the hand that wounds us, remembering that it is a sacred and loving hand; let us bow our heads and open our hearts, for it is the mercy of God visiting us. Under these painful appearances, it is our Father who comes to us, our Savior and our Friend. We can show our love by suffering for His sake and with Him, in adoration, resignation, and perfect abandonment.

St. Francis de Sales says, "Where there is less of self, there is more of God." And it is God Himself, and Jesus Christ in God, whom we can seek and find in our sufferings as in everything else.

How tenderly He will console us and what peace we shall find, when we kneel every evening at the foot of His Cross, telling Him of all our trials and failures during the past day, and perhaps also of great sorrows, always adding, "My Savior, it is Thou, and I thank Thee!"

∞

Affections

O Divine Crucified One,
through the veil of my tears, I look upon
Thy hands, pierced for the love of man;
my lips touch the nails that fastened Thy feet to
the Cross; and my hand, which embraces Thine
image, touches the wound in Thy Sacred Heart.
I have long bathed with my tears this Cross
which Thou didst bathe with Thy Blood,
and at last I have found peace.
It is as though I were sleeping upon Thy
Heart, and little by little, love has conquered
suffering. I still weep, but I weep for joy.

H. Perrèyve

∞

Examination of Conscience

• *Do I regard my sufferings from a high point of view — as a means for my purification and a gift from the goodness of God?*

• *Is Jesus the first and often the only confidant of my sorrows?*

* *Am I calm, gentle, resigned, and grateful in suffering? What was my last trial, and how did I accept it?*

* *Am I in the habit of telling Jesus before my crucifix every evening all that has annoyed me, or crossed my will, or grieved or wounded me during the day?*

∞

Resolution

∞

Spiritual Bouquet
*"We must love God alone,
with our whole heart,
and be ready to bear His Cross
as a token of His love for us."*

St. Claude de la Colombière

Step Twenty-Five

∞

Let Jesus heal your sinfulness

Jesus appeared one day to St. Mechtildis, surrounding with His arms all the Sisters who were going to Confession, purifying them, and presenting them to His Father. Afterward the saint always said to sinners, "When you have a spot upon your soul, if you wipe it off too roughly, you will cover yourself with blood without doing any good. You must take the soft material of Christ's humanity, and then you will soon wash the stain away."

This is the way to practice abandonment in our great trouble — the unbearable burden of sin.

∞

Jesus is your only refuge against sin

"Sin is the negation of love," St. Thomas says. "It interposes a distance between God and our souls." It is a complete separation between two friends who aspire to union and affection. Moreover, this abyss, once opened, can never be filled up by any human power. The offense is an infinite evil, because it is an offense against God; and any reparation we try to make is a limited one, because it comes from a creature. A divine remedy alone can cure this mortal wound. "Who can forgive sins but God only?"[217]

This good Father has never rejected one of His unhappy children. He never leaves them unless they leave Him. What words could be more touching than these: "Return, O rebellious Israel, and I will not turn my face from you, for I am holy, saith the Lord, and I will not be angry forever"?[218]

All the attributes of God are equally infinite, and under the pretext of exalting His mercy, we must not forget His justice. But in our troubled hours, it is good to remember that in all His manifestations of Himself, mercy is the chief. "His tender mercies are over all His works."[219] "The power of judging and condemning is a power which He only uses regretfully, and after long

[217]Mark 2:7.
[218]Jer. 3:12.
[219]Ps. 144:9 (RSV = Ps. 145:9).

patience with the sinner," Bossuet says. "If He condemns, it is absolutely necessary. How good He is that
it should grieve Him so much to strike man!"

When Christ came, mercy increased in one sense.
Jesus is more than "the God who, out of pure generosity, crowns poverty, saves from misfortune, and consoles grief," St. Thomas explains. "He is the pitying
Heart which suffered for sin in all its consequences, and
which spares nothing to save the human family belonging to Him."

"Behold!" said the angel of the Nativity. "I bring you
good tidings of great joy, that shall be to all the people.
For this day is born to you, in the city of David, a Savior,
who is Christ the Lord."[220] "Behold the Lamb of God,"
said St. John the Baptist, "who taketh away the sin of
the world."[221]

Christ Himself openly declared His mission: "I came
to call sinners to penance."[222] "I am the Good Shepherd:
the Good Shepherd giveth His life for His sheep."[223] "I

[220]Luke 2:10-11.
[221]John 1:29.
[222]Luke 5:32.
[223]John 10:11.

was not sent but to the sheep that are lost of the house of Israel."[224]

He loves poor sinners, not with the love of complacency, but with the love that pities. The Gospel is filled with the effusions of His Heart toward them. His most beautiful parables are for them. His tenderness overflows for the lost sheep and the prodigal son. He waits at Jacob's well for the Samaritan woman;[225] He goes to meet Zaccheus;[226] He sits at the table of publicans;[227] He pours a flood of divine love into the longing heart of the Magdalene;[228] He defends the repentant adulteress against her accusers;[229] He calls Judas His friend as He receives the kiss that betrayed Him.[230] One of His last words was a prayer for those who nailed Him to the Cross.[231] Finally, in His priests He has established "the

[224]Matt. 15:24.
[225]John 4:5 ff.
[226]Luke 19:2 ff.
[227]Luke 5:29 ff.
[228]Cf. Luke 7:37 ff.
[229]John 8:3 ff.
[230]Matt. 26:50.
[231]Luke 23:34.

ministry of reconciliation,"[232] and in the Holy Eucharist, the antidote for sin.

Well, therefore, may He call Himself "the Friend of sinners."[233] He alone can really understand their misery; He alone possesses an inexhaustible treasure of compassion. Can any sinner read the Gospel without weeping and returning love for love, without hearing the touching complaint of his Savior: "Jerusalem, Jerusalem, how often would I have gathered together thy children, as the hen doth gather her chickens under her wings; and thou wouldst not"?[234]

∞

Learn to abandon yourself
to Jesus in your sins

Frequently, after their conversion, souls are terrified by these words of Holy Scripture: "Man knoweth not whether he be worthy of love or hatred."[235] The thought of this uncertainty is a great hindrance to a real love of

[232] 2 Cor. 5:18.
[233] Matt. 11:19.
[234] Matt. 23:37.
[235] Eccles. 9:1.

God, especially when such souls are conscious of having been — perhaps for an hour, perhaps for a year, perhaps for many years — enemies of God.

Now, our loving Savior foresaw all this and gave a reply to all our anxieties, doubts, and fears. St. John Chrysostom says, "If you desire to be loved, you also must love." Let us look at Jesus. Why was it that He pardoned the Magdalene so readily and loved her so much? "Many sins are forgiven her, because she hath loved much."[236] "The more miserable we are, the more God is honored by our perfect trust in Him," says St. Claude de la Colombière.

The remission of sin may be compared to the deliverance of a criminal from prison. Jesus is waiting for him at the gate and receives him with open arms. Their joy is mutual, for we are told, "There shall be joy in Heaven upon one sinner that doth penance, more than upon ninety-nine just who need not penance."[237] Origen says, "The day of a man's conversion and the hour of his pardon is a festival day for Jesus Christ." Jesus has mourned over his obstinacy in sin; He is glad when the sinner

[236]Luke 7:47.
[237]Luke 15:7.

brings his sins to the feet of his Lord and pleads for forgiveness. If it were not for our sins, He would not be a Savior.

One Christmas night, St. Jerome wished to give a present to the infant Jesus. First, he offered the Lord his works on the Holy Scripture; then his labors for the conversion of souls to a more perfect life; then his own virtues, if there were any to offer. But all this was not what our Savior wanted. "Jerome," He said, "it is thy sins I wish for. Give them to me, so that I may pardon them."

Do all in your power to purify your soul. Then practice love, simplicity, and filial abandonment, because there is a more real repentance in perfect trust than in any other action. "In our satisfaction for sin," St. Thomas explains, "it is not the quantity nor the multiplicity of interior or exterior acts that count, but the strength and fullness of our love." St. Ignatius says, "If the enemy tries to depress us, we must lift up our souls in faith and hope to our Lord, considering the love and the Heart that is waiting to save us."

Listen to these words of St. Claude de la Colombière: "All the evil you have ever done is nothing in comparison to the wrong you do our Lord by not trusting Him."

Moreover, is this constant dwelling on past sin always quite sincere or consistent? Some souls are continually lamenting and asking themselves, "Has God really pardoned me?" Their anxiety is not very deep. If a few words of reassurance are said to them, they are happy again.

When Magdalene was pardoned, her life was completely changed. It became a life of penance, austerities, and prayer — a life of heroic perfection. She thirsted to make reparation for years of sin. She became a living proof of the reality of her conversion and the sincerity of her love. Do we resemble her in the slightest degree?

"Infinite Goodness opens its arms so wide that it can embrace all those who seek refuge there."[238] St. Alphonsus Liguori advised troubled souls to make use of this aspiration: "O my God, if for me there can never be forgiveness, remember that I am nonetheless Thine and shall be Thine forever!"

∞

Affections
O heavenly Physician of my soul and
sovereign Remedy for all my evils,

---

[238]Dante, *The Divine Comedy*, "*Purgatorio*," cant. 3.

I present myself before Thee as
a sick person despairing of any other
help but from Thy loving Heart
Thou canst, if Thou wilt,
heal all my infirmities.

For my part, I am ready to
employ the fire and sword of entire
mortification and crucifixion of self.

O my charitable Physician,
be my loving Remedy.

St. Margaret Mary

∞

Examination of Conscience
• *Am I troubled by anxiety about past sins?*

• *Do I have, before all things, perfect trust in God?*

• *Do I go to Jesus as to a merciful*
Savior, a kind Physician?

• *Am I really in peace after a good confession?*
Do I try to atone for the past by my
fidelity, love, and penance now?

• *What are my practices of austerity,*
mortification, and expiation?

A Pocket Retreat for Catholics

∞

Resolution

∞

Spiritual Bouquet

"When a soul only receives me as a Friend,
I allow her to become sick, in order that
she may call upon me as a Physician."

Our Lord to St. Gertrude

Step Twenty-Six

∞

*Let your imperfections
draw you closer to Jesus*

"No one will ever be so holy in this life as to be free from
all imperfections. We must not lie down; also, we must
not imagine we can fly, for we are only little chickens
that do not yet have the use of their wings. The more we
realize our own misery, the more we shall confide in the
mercy of God. God does not love our imperfections, but
He loves us with a tender love in spite of our imperfections." These words of St. Francis de Sales teach us that
we must abandon ourselves to Jesus in our imperfections
and make use of these imperfections to love Him more.

∞

Your imperfections must not discourage you
The gentle Bishop of Geneva, so appropriately
called the "encouraging Doctor," said, "We must live

and die between two pillows: that of our own misery and that of trust in God." Such abandonment requires of us, first of all, never to be astonished at our faults, and also never to give way to discouragement on account of our own weakness. We must take care of ourselves patiently and resign ourselves to live as "incurables," so far as our spirituality is concerned.

St. Francis de Sales says, "When you commit sins, do not be astonished. It is nothing to wonder at, that infirmity should be infirm, or weakness weak, or misery miserable. We must have patience with ourselves, because we are human and not angelic. We shall never be quite cured until we are in Paradise. The maladies of our heart, as well as those of our body, come on horseback, galloping posthaste; but they leave us on foot, walking very slowly." Our evil inclinations always remain within us — at least the germ of them remains — and no one can, unless by a special privilege of grace, such as the Church recognizes in the Blessed Virgin Mary, ever avoid falling into indeliberate venial sins.

Moreover, the sight of our faults is very useful in maintaining within us a knowledge of ourselves and great humility. How, indeed, can we trust in our own strength, or think ourselves of any importance, when we are overcome by the first wind of temptation, when we see our good resolutions breaking down, and vanishing away? St. John Chrysostom says: "Often the Devil himself is of great use to us; only we must know how to use him to our own advantage." Imperfections are so many windows through which the light streams more abundantly upon our own miseries.

God looks tenderly upon humility and bestows His grace upon the humble in proportion to their self-abasement. "A chariot full of good works, driven by Pride, is bound for Hell," says St. Gregory of Nyssa,[239] "but driven by Humility, it takes the road to Heaven."

The most important point is never to be discouraged. "We are saved by hope."[240] "This virtue is like a strong chain let down from Heaven, drawing our souls thither," says St. John Chrysostom. "If we hold fast to it, it will draw us up to sublime heights; but the soul which gives way to despondency, and casts aside this holy anchor, will soon fall into sin and perish in the abyss of evil. The enemy knows this and fills our hearts with despairing thoughts, heavier than lead."

[239]St. Gregory of Nyssa (c. 330-c. 395), Bishop of Nyssa.
[240]Rom. 8:24.

We should act as the laborer acts. He has foreseen that evil weeds will spring up in his field, so he husbands his strength so that he may be able to root them out when the proper time comes. Instead of crawling wearily along, discontented with ourselves, and almost with God, we shall take heart, and begin again to walk in the path of perfection, "rejoicing that we are a good piece of work for the good God," says St. Francis de Sales. In such dispositions as these, and with the grace of God, we shall certainly make progress; for, as St. Ignatius says, "that which a careless person acquires with much labor in many years, a fervent soul gains easily in a short time."

∞

Learn to make use of your imperfections

Our first resolution, when we are conscious of our imperfections, must be to fight actively against them; then, when we have seriously engaged in this struggle, it will strengthen us to remember that we are not alone, but that God is fighting with us, encouraging and supporting our efforts, because He knows our weakness.

"The child who falls as soon as he leaves his mother, and tries to walk alone, returns to her with more love than ever to be comforted for the hurt he has inflicted upon himself," says Père Grou.[241] "The lesson he learns from his fall is that he must never leave his mother. The experience of his own weakness, and the tenderness with which his mother receives him, inspire him with more affection for that loving mother."

We also return to our friendship with our good Master and throw ourselves into that divine Heart, which St. Gertrude so justly called "the hospital for all who suffer." Our very faults bring us back to Him who is the only one who can help us to perfection. St. Francis de Sales says, "If you fall, if you encounter some new difficulty or trouble, it is only to make you stand more faithfully on your guard and call upon your Father in Heaven to help you."

Another practice of abandonment and confidence is to make an offering every evening of all the sins and shortcomings of the day, "to throw them like a log of wood at the feet of our Savior, so that they may be consumed in the fire of His mercy," as St. Claude de la Colombière says.

---

[241] Jean Nicholas Grou (1731-1803), French Jesuit and spiritual writer.

This was the practice of the pious author of the *Imitation of Christ:* "Lord, I offer to Thee all my sins and offenses that I have committed in Thy sight, and in that of the holy angels, that Thou mayest burn and consume them in the fire of Thy charity, and mayest blot out all the stains of my sins . . . fully pardoning all, and mercifully receiving me to the kiss of peace."[242]

Not that our infidelities and imperfections can ever be pleasing to our Savior, but He has always an unquenchable thirst to absolve and cure us. Our confessions at the feet of this, the first of all priests, have the most purifying effects. Indeed, if every voluntary remembrance of a past sin, when we still excuse it and approve of it, is a still more grievous sin, so it is only just that new merits should reward the newly absolved soul whenever it condemns, regrets, and forsakes its sins.

Jesus once asked this offering from a saint: "Gather together all your spurious incense, your false myrrh, your false gold — i.e., your prayers full of distractions, your imperfect mortifications, your good works so stained and spoiled by your natural inclinations. Offer them to me with repentance and love, and I

[242]*Imitation of Christ,* Bk. 4, ch. 9, no. 2.

will transform them all into pearls." We who fall so many times during the day should every evening throw ourselves and our miseries into the burning furnace of the Heart of Jesus. Thus, being set free from sin, "we shall make up for lost time by quickening our footsteps," says St. Francis de Sales.

∞

Affections

O most generous Love, behold me, a miserable human creature, tempest-tossed by the winds of my many infidelities to Thee. I come to seek refuge under the wings of Thine infinite compassion. If Thou dost not help me, I can never find rest.

My Jesus, supply by Thine own goodness for all my negligences. O faithful Guide of my pilgrimage, support my steps, so that I may joyfully enter Thy glorious tabernacle.

St. Gertrude

∞

Examination of Conscience
• *Do I accept as an expiation the state of humility in which my many imperfections leave me? Do I remain calm and brave, instead of feeling annoyed and irritated?*

+ *Do I try with all my heart to correct myself,
never forgetting that I ought to strive for perfection?*

+ *Do I trust in Jesus and not in myself?*

+ *Am I going to try every evening to make an
offering of my sins and imperfections to Jesus?*

∞

Resolution

∞

Spiritual Bouquet
*"Weakness is not such a very great evil,
if only we have enough fidelity and courage
to correct ourselves gradually."*

St. Francis de Sales

Step Twenty-Seven

∞

Rely on Jesus in your adoration and your reparation

Who has not been obliged to confess, with many tears, and often in the midst of temptations to despair of self, his own helplessness and insufficiency? It is the special cross of every soul when brought face-to-face with personal difficulties. Our Lord especially wishes us to confess this helplessness to Him. He expressly tells us, "Without me, you can do nothing."[243]

Fortunately we have the answer of the apostle St. Paul: "I can do all things in Him who strengtheneth me."[244] When our own strength fails, Jesus is sufficient for us. St. Ignatius tells us, "The Lord our God supplies for all our deficiencies."

[243]John 15:5.
[244]Phil. 4:13.

Let us meditate on the name that a pious soul gave to our Savior: "He is the Divine Sufficiency for us" — first, for adoration and then for reparation.

∞

You must unite your adoration with Christ's

"Thou art my Divine Sufficiency," said Mother Marie de Sales Chappuis. "Of myself, I am poor in the sight of God, but with Him I am rich. When I confess my insufficiency, I acknowledge the sufficiency of God." This is borrowed from St. Paul: "Our sufficiency is from God."[245]

Our good Master has not been satisfied with becoming the food of our souls. He consoles our hearts by inundating them with the overflowing waters of His divine love. He has established one more bond between our souls and Himself — another communion. He desires that we should have need of Him — of His help, His strength, and His protection — for the accomplishment of all our duties. He cannot allow us to be isolated from Him in any of the labors to which our life on earth exposes us, or in the necessity imposed upon us of preparing for the life to come.

[245] 2 Cor. 3:5.

The first of our duties with regard to God is adoration. To be a creature means that we must depend upon our Creator; we must acknowledge our Master; we must resign ourselves to be consumed for His glory, and adoration is the most perfect homage of the creature to his Creator. When we wish to adore God, we have only the absolute incapacity of finite beings, and the most holy souls, who, "like larks, sing more sweetly the higher they ascend," are soon obliged to "fly lower, and cease from singing," because they know "that God is above all praise," says St. Francis de Sales.

The true worshiper of the Father was Jesus. His life on earth was one perpetual adoration of His Father, and His exterior life was passed in forming for Himself those who "adore God in spirit and in truth."[246] He cannot act without our cooperation. He has accomplished, for Himself and for us, every act of sublime adoration, because we are for Him "the fullness of Him who is filled all in all."[247] The religion that He taught is for all time — from one eternity to another, from the beginning of Creation to the crowning point of man, and the angels,

[246] John 4:24.
[247] Eph. 1:23.

and Mary, who was the head of all His wonderful works. "He Himself supplies for all that is wanting in His creatures," says St. Mechtildis, and this God, who is so infinitely adorable, is infinitely adored by Jesus, who alone can infinitely adore His Father.

Therefore we need only offer to God the homage of Jesus, and our own poor homage with His: "To Him who is the only perfect man, and whose infinite perfection supplies for our deficiencies," says Bossuet. The priest who, every morning, with the hands of Christ, elevates the Sacred Host and pronounces the words "Through Him [i.e., Jesus], with Him, in Him . . . all glory and honor is yours, Almighty Father," pays off our debt of adoration. "The Lamb that was slain" is equal to Him "who sitteth upon the throne forever and ever."[248]

Every Christian "whose soul is at peace with God is an altar," says St. Augustine, and in a lesser degree, but in reality, says Origen, "he is a true priest." Jesus is, in all the members of His Body, the universal Priest of His Father. Let us therefore unite our voices to His voice — "the King of all voices," as St. Francis de Sales says, the voice of our prayers, our good works, our desires, and

[248] Apoc. 5:12-13 (RSV = Rev. 5:12-13).

our whole life — and then we shall have sufficiently fulfilled our chief duty of adoration.

∞

Jesus makes reparation for your sins

Another obligation for all Christians is reparation. Our life is indeed the imitation, or, rather, the continuation, of the life of Christ within our souls as members of His Mystical Body.

The Incarnation was a work of reparation; Christ became our Redeemer, and He still remains upon our altars. It is necessary, then, that we also should be victims devoted to the glory of His Father and the salvation of the world; that we should present our bodies and souls to the Savior "as a living sacrifice," to share with Him in the accomplishment of His Passion. Reparation becomes a necessity to pious souls.

God requires "a living sacrifice, holy, pleasing unto God."[249] As a creature, and a sinner, man can offer only a limited reparation. As Bossuet says, "No one can offer the price of our redemption except the Holy One of God." Jesus Himself came to our assistance, "the High

[249]Rom. 12:1.

Priest, holy, innocent, undefiled, separated from sinners . . . who needeth not daily, as the other priests, to offer sacrifices for His own sins."[250]

Our Lord said to St. Margaret Mary, "I am thy security: I will pay for thee." He pays for us; He sold Himself to redeem us. The Infant in the manger was already wearing His crown of thorns. The youth at Nazareth was already bending under the weight of His Cross. The Master, in the days of His public life, His parables, His Beatitudes, His miracles, His journeys, bringing comfort and help to all, was always, in His Heart, the Martyr of Calvary, dying to save the world and avenge the divine honor.

The Holy Eucharist and the Sacrifice of the Mass continue this work of salvation and reparation. It is also continued in the martyrs and saints, and in the thousand forms of suffering by which we all "fill up the measure of the sufferings of Christ."[251]

Once, in a large family, one of the sons was seized with kleptomania. Everything he saw attracted his attention and excited his covetousness; he stole, carried

[250]Cf. Heb. 7:26-27.
[251]Cf. Col. 1:24.

away his stolen property, and so exposed himself to disgrace and the severe justice of his country. Naturally, his father was much distressed, offended, and dishonored by such conduct. He sent a servant in pursuit of this poor madman, with instructions to excuse him, and make reparation for the evils he had done during his madness.

It is thus that our good God has acted with regard to us. We are His children by adoption. Jesus is His own Son, the Son of His Heart, and it was Jesus "who took upon Himself the form of a servant,"[252] to be our security for all our sinful actions, which are indeed real acts of folly.

"God embraces the guilty for the sake of His own innocent Son," Bossuet tells us. Being fed with the perfection of Christ, it is He whom we offer up in our sacrifices, upon the altar of our churches, and upon the altar of our hearts. He is at the same time Priest and Victim, and when God looks upon the face of His Christ, He also looks upon the contrite and humble heart of the sinner who repents.

Let us appeal to Him confidently when we approach the tribunal of Penance, when we receive absolution,

[252]Cf. Phil. 2:7.

and whenever we perform any act of mortification, either willingly and by our own choice, or as imposed upon us by Divine Providence.

∞

Affections
Into the golden censer of Thy divine Heart, in which burns forever the perfume of Thine eternal love, I cast my heart as a tiny grain of incense. May Thy Spirit of Life deign to kindle it, and consume it, for Thy glory.

I present to Thee, O most adorable Father, Thy most humble Son. The love of His Heart has most fully supplied for all my shortcomings. The purity of His spotless life has atoned for all the evil that I have ever committed in thought, word, and deed. His perfection has supplied for all my imperfections.

St. Mechtildis and St. Gertrude

∞

Examination of Conscience
✦ *Do I really think seriously of my duties as a creature to my Creator?*

✦ *As I can never offer Him any act of adoration that is worthy of Him, do I call upon Jesus to help me?*

Rely on Jesus in your adoration

• *What do I do in reparation for my personal sins?
Do I have recourse to Jesus, offering Him, in compensation
for my sins, His own labors, tears, sufferings, and death?*

• *During Holy Mass, do I unite myself with the divine
Victim, who is making reparation for us all?*

∞

Resolution

∞

Spiritual Bouquet
*"My Heart will supply for all thy deficiencies.
It shall atone for thee and shall acquit
thee of all thine obligations."*

Our Blessed Lord to St. Margaret Mary

Step Twenty-Eight

∞

Offer prayers and thanksgiving through Jesus

"If you ask the Father anything in my name, He will give it to you."[253]

In these words of our dear Lord, we find the key to all heavenly treasures. We can no longer have any doubts or hesitation or discouragement. We are quite certain that the door will open to us when we knock, if we rely upon the promise of our Savior.

In proportion as we stand before Him, as poor, weak creatures, "having nothing and possessing all things,"[254] so He will be to us our Divine Sufficiency, first for prayer and then for thanksgiving.

[253]John 16:23.
[254]2 Cor. 6:10.

∞

Jesus prays within you

All Christians are united to Jesus Christ because of the sacrament of holy Baptism, which makes them His members and associates them with His life and spirit — so much so that every action of the God-Man has become universal. The same is true of His prayer. Jesus Christ never prayed for Himself alone; He prayed for us all, because we are the members of His Body. "I pray for them [i.e., in their favor and in their place]. And not for them only do I pray, but for them also who, through their word, shall believe in me."[255] "My prayers are in their prayers; their prayers shall have, according to their faith, the same value as mine." St. Augustine says, "It is Christ, our Head, who prays within us." And for this reason, all the prayers of the Church conclude with the words: "Through Jesus Christ, our Lord."

He has revealed His will to us by giving us, in the Lord's Prayer, the formula most pleasing to Him. "To pray to God alone," says St. Cyprian, "is the form of prayer most familiar and most loving; when the Father hears the very words of His Son, surely He will be

[255]John 17:9, 20.

touched by them. If we pray in His own words, we do indeed pray in His name."

When St. Teresa, the model for all souls who wish to pray well, knelt down to pray, she recollected herself for a moment and then imagined she was with the Apostles and listening to our Lord when He said, "Thus, therefore, shall you pray."[256]

This is why the prayers of the saints have so much power with God, because they pray with faith, hope, trust, and perfect abandonment to Him who is "always living to make intercession for us."[257]

When God listens to us, He hears only the voice of His beloved Son, in whom alone He is well pleased. It is really "the spirit of adoption of sons, whereby we cry, 'Abba, Father.' "[258]

Let us, then, make use of this loving Heart, which desires only to spend itself entirely for us. Let this Heart be the medium of our prayers and desires. We shall be sure to ask well, and to ask for what is good for us, and consequently, our prayers will be answered if we

[256] Matt. 6:9.
[257] Heb. 7:25.
[258] Rom. 8:15.

ask in the words that give pleasure to our Father in Heaven.

There is no better proof of a Christian life than the habit of prayer, with the full conviction of our own insufficiency and a firm faith in the sufficiency of our Savior. When we can truthfully say, "I pray, but it is not I who pray; it is Jesus who prays in me," we are not very far from saying, "I live, now not I, but Christ liveth in me."[259] He is the principle of all my thoughts, feelings, and actions. He is indeed the soul of my spiritual life.

∞

Jesus assists your thanksgiving

Our life, as far as we are concerned, an abyss of necessities; it is an ocean of benefits on the part of God, "from whom all goodness flows upon His creatures," as St. Ignatius says. His great gifts are Creation, Redemption, the Holy Eucharist, and Heaven — four words, the depths of which we have only to penetrate to understand how good God is. Moreover, if each individual soul recalls his interior history, if he is able to follow

[259]Gal. 2:20.

within himself, year by year and day by day, the footsteps of God, he will be overwhelmed by the weight of
divine largess.

"When we are grateful, we love," says St. Augustine.
This is why the Holy Scriptures, especially the Psalms
and the apostolic letters, when referring to our practice
of the virtues of religion, recommend so often and so
strongly the practice of thanksgiving. It also explains,
as St. John Chrysostom says, why the solemn and precious mysteries celebrated in our churches bear the
name of *Eucharist* ("thanksgiving"), because they are
the memorial of the gifts of God and the subject of our
thanksgivings.

Souls able to understand the extent of this duty of
gratitude never fail to observe, at the same time, their
own powerlessness to fulfill it as it should be fulfilled.
St. Gertrude was one of those souls who lived in closest
union with our Lord, and she often exclaimed, "Conde-
scend, O my Jesus, whom I love so much, to fulfill for
me this act of thanksgiving to the fullest extent of justice and love."

St. John Chrysostom says, "Because man so often
fails in this obligation of gratitude, the Son of God puts
Himself in our place and takes from His own treasures

all that is necessary to do for us what we can never do ourselves."

A very simple soul always prayed and gave thanks in this admirable formula: "Eternal Father, I ask of Thee this favor through the merits of Thy divine Son. Take His divine merits, pay Thyself, and give me the rest." What could be truer and more beautiful than this prayer? Indeed, as the merits of our Lord are infinite, when God has paid all our debts with this treasure, which is ours, there still remains an infinite treasure for another time.

Our Savior, wishing to be one with us, prays, loves, and gives thanks with us, in us, and for us, and we are able to make His acts of thanksgiving our own.

∞

Affections

I owe Thee honor, love, adoration, and
thanksgiving, and I owe my whole self
to Thee for an infinity of reasons. I have
nothing with which to pay all my debts to Thee,
for I am nothing and possess nothing of my own.

But behold the divine Heart of Thy beloved Son,
which Thou hast given to me. I offer it to Thee

Offer prayers through Jesus

*to praise Thee, to thank Thee, and to beg of Thee
all the graces that are still necessary for my salvation.*

St. John Eudes

∞

Examination of Conscience

• *Am I perfectly aware of my own helplessness
in asking favors and giving thanks for them?*

• *Am I careful always to pray in union with Jesus and
ask only that which He can ask with me and for me?*

• *Is my favorite prayer the Our Father? And how do I recite it?*

• *Do I ask my good Savior to give thanks for me?*

• *Do I not often forget the duty of gratitude for
my vocation and for all my other graces?*

∞

Resolution

∞

Spiritual Bouquet
*"I appoint thee to be the heiress
and guardian of all the treasures of
my Heart — in time and eternity."*

Our Lord to St. Margaret Mary

Step Twenty-Nine

∞

Find holiness and happiness in Jesus

A pious soul, continually laboring actively and energetically in the work of her perfection, was wont to encourage herself in following Jesus by these words of humility: "I have no virtues; but Jesus is mine, and He has them all." That is to say, I have nothing of my own, but the grace of God is with me to sustain my will and to bless my efforts; I have a finished model to reproduce, a perfect pattern, by which to regulate my life; when I approach His throne with confidence and hope, I have at my disposal a merciful and always seasonable assistance.

Another faithful soul loved to say, "Thou hast taken the place of everyone and everything with me. Thou art my treasure, my country, and my only love. My sole possession is Thyself."

Heaven is peopled with saints and blessed ones, and as this earth is the preparation and the "rough sketch" for Heaven, so God, when He makes His dwelling place within our souls, brings us at the same time that beginning of glory which sows within us the seeds of perfect holiness and beatitude.

Hence, it follows that our Savior is indeed our Divine Sufficiency, first for holiness and then for happiness.

∽

Holiness springs from union with Jesus

The holiness of God is God's union with Himself, so He finds within Himself all that is necessary and perfect. The holiness of creatures is an imitation of this perfection of God. "Holiness is well-ordered love," says St. Augustine; "in its last analysis, it consists in the perfect love of God," adds Pope Leo XIII, causing us to cling to God in such a manner that the words of St. Paul become true: "He who is joined to the Lord is one spirit."[260]

This brings us back to our first point: that holiness is a life of union with God; the life of Jesus has become our life. This means that we are so penetrated by His divine grace, so enlightened by His light, so devoted to His will, so dependent upon His guidance, so conformed

[260] 1 Cor. 6:17.

to His ideas, so completely in sympathy with all His tastes and affections, so open to receive His gifts, so devoted to His interests, and so docile to His good pleasure that at last we become completely possessed by Him, and have henceforth no real life or independence of our own.

Such an attainment appears to us immense and very distant. The struggle for perfection would discourage the bravest souls if, in the midst of all their labors, they did not support their own weakness by the all-sufficiency of their Savior. Our Lord made this promise one day to a confidante of His, St. Margaret Mary: "Thou shalt never fail to receive assistance until my own power fails."

He called Himself "the way":[261] He is the road that leads to Heaven. He — the Master and Model of all virtue — has shown by His life, and revealed in His Gospel, the means of our perfection. The teaching of His Church explains them, and His saints put them in practice. To enter on the way of salvation, we must follow Jesus and mold our lives upon the pattern of this divine Model.

[261] John 14:6.

A serious and thorough examination, as much as may be useful, of all our thoughts, affections, and actions will soon reveal to us whether we are really in this way of life, if we are really acting as the saints act, through Him, in Him, and with Him; that is to say, with the help of His grace and in accordance with His teaching.

"Through Him": it is He who enlightens us, purifies us, and finally places us safely in the arms of His Father. Through Him, we receive grace, pardon, and all the help we need. Through Him, we find God, or find Him again, if we have forsaken Him, and it is He who will at last introduce us into the kingdom of Heaven.

"With Him": He is the Companion of our journey, the Friend, the Spouse, the Food. Wherever I go, except when I sin, He is with me: in my work and in my sleep, in prayer and in love, in joy and in grief, in life and in death, He is my All in All. And in Heaven, I shall be forever with the Lord.

"In Him": this is the crown of union — to have truly but one heart and one soul with Him. He invites me, draws me to Himself, receives me, and loves me with an eternal love. I enter into the depths of His thought, His life, and His love. I share His labors; I cooperate in His work. He gives me everything, and it is Heaven on earth when I rest in His Heart.

It is indeed true that we would soon become saints if we passed our whole life in this Way, if all our actions were done only "through Jesus, with Him, and in Him." St. Ignatius says, "It is this of which I am assured, by that infinite goodness which is in Him so magnificently communicative of all His gifts and favors; and of that eternal love of His, which is always more ready to give us holiness than we are to desire it."

∞

Jesus is the source of happiness

"Our dear Lord," explains St. Francis de Sales, "to attract souls to Himself, gives them, as it were, little specimens and samples of the happiness of our true country. We can scarcely judge of the real quality of a thing by a small sample of it, but these foretastes of celestial joys serve to kindle the desire for Heaven within our souls."

"The whole end and aim of man is to be happy," says Bossuet. "Jesus Christ only came to give us the means of attaining happiness. When we find our happiness in true joys, it is the source of all good, and the source of all evil is to fix our hearts on forbidden joys."

"Happiness is the conquest and possession of the Sovereign Good," St. Thomas tells us. "The Sovereign Good — infinite, eternal, and unique — is the true God; it is Jesus Christ alone, dwelling with the Father and the Holy Spirit." Therefore, happiness for each one of us consists in the conquest and possession of Jesus, in time first, and then in eternity. Always and everywhere the Heart of Jesus is the Paradise of our hearts.

"What we call happiness in this world," says Msgr. de Ségur, "is the conquest and possession of all that is good, desirable, and agreeable in the purely natural order; as, for instance, the pleasure of family affections, of tender and faithful friendship, temporal prosperity lawfully acquired, good health, success in our efforts, and a good reputation. Happiness is, in one word, all that is pleasant and good. But these sources of happiness, real as they seem to be, have little consistency unless they lean upon real joy — that is to say, upon true piety — and consequently, upon our Lord and Savior, Jesus Christ. When we possess real piety, Jesus, the Sovereign Good, will not allow secondary and relative pleasures to spoil us. He maintains them in all their goodness. He elevates and strengthens them; He sanctifies and deifies them by uniting them with Himself. Also, with Him, all the bitterness and suffering of this present life are easily forgotten; resting upon His divine Heart, we soon find consolation for all disappointments. With Him, we learn how to suffer patiently, and even joyfully. The Christian and the saint carry Jesus with them on their journey through this world, and their 'light shines before men' as a living sacrament of the 'peace of God, and pure and celestial joy.'"

The only way, then, to be really happy is to be holy and live in union with Jesus. "Our paradise," exclaims St. Bernard, "is Thyself, O Christ my Lord; all is ill with me where Thou art not."

In the spiritual life, there are sometimes moments when we feel a void in our hearts, but this sadness comes always from one cause: it is because He who can suffice for all is not occupying our heart sufficiently; He is not sufficiently living within us; we do not clasp Him tightly enough in our arms or embrace Him with our deepest affections. "As soon as God has taken entire possession of our soul," says St. Ignatius, "no one can take away from us our divine treasure without our consent; there is no longer anything in the events of this life that ought to distress us or cause us much pain."

∞

Affections

O Jesus, gate of Paradise,
O Jesus, gate that leads to God,
expansion and entrance into the
Heart of God from this earth of ours,
to realize Thy greatness and to know indeed who
Thou art is enough to make us holy and happy.
To be able always to say, "Through Him, with Him,
and in Him," is sufficient to make us strong,
to keep us chaste, to help us to wait for everything
and to possess everything; but, above all things,
it is sufficient to make us love Thee
with our whole heart.

Msgr. Gay

∞

Examination of Conscience

• *Have I decided to be holy in my vocation,*
whatever it may be, and to make any
sacrifice so that I may follow Jesus?

• *Am I going to try to perform all my*
actions in union with Jesus?
Am I now really united to Him?
If not, what is my state?

Find holiness and happiness in Jesus

* *What are the joys that I seek after now?*
What is the happiness I hope for in the future?

* *Do I rejoice in being a real friend of Jesus?*

    * *Am I in a state of grace, with a
desire to become more holy?*

    * *Do I have any satisfaction or
desire that Jesus cannot bless?*

∞

Resolution

∞

Spiritual Bouquet
*"Live, and live forever,
my beloved Jesus, Thou holiness of
my soul and paradise of my heart!"*

Blessed Colombini

Step Thirty

∞

Prepare now for union with God in Heaven

A little child once asked Almighty God in all simplicity, "O my dear Father, do the little children in Heaven sleep in a cradle or in your arms?" "In my arms," replied the Lord. This is what death really is and what it should be to us all.

Our life of union with God on earth is only a rough sketch, dimly seen, of what it will be hereafter. Its perfection and crown is in Heaven. "I shall be satisfied when Thy glory shall appear,"[262] O Jesus, and death will be for me the gate of life.

Let us now meditate, first, on our meeting with our dear Savior and, second, on the life of union in Heaven.

[262]Ps. 16:15 (RSV = Ps. 17:15).

∞

*Death will bring you
face-to-face with Jesus*

The day of our meeting with Jesus will be the day
of our death. True Christians call this moment the
hour of their birth, because it is then that we die to
this world and enter upon our true life. "For we know
if our earthly house of this habitation is dissolved, that
we have a building of God, a house not made with hands,
eternal in Heaven. While we are in the body, we are absent from the Lord. Therefore, we have a good will to
be absent rather from the body, and to be present with
the Lord."[263]

"If death is the masterpiece of divine justice, it is
equally the masterpiece of God's love," says Lacordaire.
And Pope Leo XIII says, "He loved us when He gave
us life; He loves us also when He takes away our life."
The Gospel announces the death of our Savior in these
simple words: "His hour was come that He should pass
out of this world to the Father."[264] As for ourselves, Père
Tissot, a holy religious who had preached often, and

[263]Cf. 2 Cor. 5:1, 6, 8.
[264]John 13:1.

faithfully practiced, union with our Lord, said, "Death is like the leap of a little child into his mother's arms."

During this life, man, the beloved son who came from the Heart of God, plays, grows to maturity, labors, sleeps, prays, and suffers. Then there comes a day when this great God, who is both Father and Master, decides that the trial of His creature has lasted long enough, so He calls him to Himself and holds out His arms. One last effort, and the creature is at rest upon the Heart of his Creator. The just man regards death as the moment when God will take him down from his cross and receive him into His fatherly arms, there to enjoy eternal beatitude. "The Father of all comes to seek His children in order that where He is, there we may be also," says Bossuet.

Such is the consoling vision opened up to us by divine Love: at the end of all our trials is Jesus. It was His will also to die; not being able to suffer in detail the trials of all His members, He accepted death — the summary of them all, the culminating point. In death, He is still with us, and still remains our Way to the true life. As a friend would follow without hesitation his dearest friend whose hand he was holding, even through the darkness of the blackest subterranean passage, certain of soon issuing into the light of day and pure air, so does the Christian, who leans upon Jesus Christ when traversing the dark valley of the shadow of death.

"He who fears to see his Savior does not love Him," says St. Augustine. This is why His true friends love death, and even desire it. St. Paul was weary of living; he "desired to be dissolved and to be with Christ."[265] "I cannot live without Him," said St. Teresa. "I will gladly die to see Him." St. Francis of Assisi said, "How welcome and beloved art thou, my sister Death!" Finally, St. Ambrose wrote a whole treatise called *The Blessing of Death* and summed up the thought of all those who love and desire death in these words: "I do not fear death, because I know that I shall be confided to the care of a good Master and shall be safe in His mercy."

When on earth God has been our sole happiness, death is the kiss and consummation of charity, and for him who has communicated almost daily, death, sweet and holy death, is the beginning of an eternal Communion; we pass from the eucharistic life to the fullness of the life of God.

[265] Cf. 2 Cor. 5:8; Phil. 1:23.

"Life is really one long act of patience, and death is our entrance into eternal joy," says St. Bernard. "The Christian dies singing and sings as he dies." In that supreme hour, he places his whole hope in Jesus, having always been the object of His great compassion and infinite mercy. Whether just or justified, innocent or penitent, we know that "the souls of the just are in the hand of God, and that the torment of death shall not touch them."[266] We have only to accomplish this last duty generously, to trust entirely, to abandon ourselves wholly, and to say to our best friend, "Open to me, Lord Jesus, open to me."

∞

Union with Jesus on earth leads
to union with Him in Heaven

"Walk in love, as Christ also hath loved us."[267] Such is, indeed, the will of our divine Lord: these meditations have taught it clearly. Already our hearts are more at ease, and happier, for while He promises us Heaven for all eternity, God also desires that we should already

[266]Wisd. 3:1.
[267]Eph. 5:2.

find a Heaven on earth. It is God's joy to act toward us as He wished to do at first, before sin entered the world.

Where does this way of love lead us? From union on earth to eternal union in Heaven. The happiness of Heaven is nothing but a great familiarity with God, carried to a degree far beyond any human conception. "Every grace that we receive here is only the seed of that which will exist forever in glory," says St. Thomas. And St. Alphonsus Liguori says, "Perfect charity with the blessed will take the form which our love took during our journey through this life." When he enters Heaven, the Christian will not change his heart; he will have the same heart, only it will be exquisitely perfected. *There* Jesus gives Himself in proportion as He has been comprehended, desired, and loved *here*.

"Whatever has been begun on earth will be continued in eternity," says Bossuet. Special glories and joys are reserved for the meek, the chaste, the lovers of the Cross — for martyrs, doctors, virgins, and penitents. It is as the Holy Spirit says: "Because his soul hath labored, he shall see and be filled."[268]

[268]Isa. 53:11.

The Blessed Virgin Mary has special rights to a special love, which can be claimed only by a mother, just as during our Lord's infancy, she allowed Him to caress her with a tenderness reserved only for a mother. "How many kisses He gave St. Joseph with His blessed mouth," St. Francis de Sales says; therefore, in Heaven, St. Joseph also has special privileges. St. John leaned upon His breast; Magdalene, the great model for all penitents, afterward "chose the better part";[269] St. Teresa heard Him say to her, "I am the Jesus of Teresa." St. Rose of Lima was affianced to Him — He said to her, "Be the bride of my Heart." St. Anthony of Padua held Him in his arms. When St. Gerard Majella[270] was a child, Mary gave the child Jesus from her arms to play with him. St. Gertrude, St. Mechtildis, St. Margaret Mary, and countless other saints, have penetrated into His secrets and listened to the confidences of His divine Heart.

In Heaven, these familiar and close relations are not merely very sweet memories; in privileged souls, they created vocations, necessities, capacities, and habits of

[269]Luke 10:42.

[270]St. Gerard Majella (d. 1755), lay brother and patron saint of childbirth and expectant mothers.

union that the state of glory crowns and satisfies. St. Thomas says, "In proportion as I have known Jesus and loved Him, so will He give Himself to me."

Thus, the soul who walks on earth in the way of union becomes the Benjamin whom God will bless in this world, and in the other. Those who, "being prisoners of His love and grace," as St. Ignatius says, have lived in perfect trust in Him, abandonment, perseverance, and love, even when faith seemed most difficult, will be loved more dearly in the light of glory. In Christ, then, at last revealed to them, given, and possessed, they will see, hear, and enjoy all the beauty and love that are to be the eternal reward of those who have abandoned themselves without reserve to Him. In the past, their greatest happiness was to give pleasure to their Savior.

"In Heaven, close to that Heart, whereon we shall see our names written in letters of gold," as St. Francis de Sales says, our canticle of thanksgiving will be this: "I could never have believed that my good God was so good."

And then those words of Jesus that have served as the basis of all these meditations will never pass away. He will say to us forever, "Abide in my love" — that is, in closest union with me.

Prepare now for union in Heaven

∞

Affections

O Jesus, Thy love has set me free;
lead me home to Thyself.
It is Thine own kingdom, O Christ,
and it is henceforth mine also.
I wish to see it all; hide nothing from me.
On earth, I was a beggar;
here I am intoxicated with joy.
O my King, Thy goodness and beauty
are too much for me; my voice fails me,
except to say, "I thank Thee."

Père Tissot

∞

Examination of Conscience
• *Do I have an exaggerated fear of death?*
Am I going to try for the future to look upon death as
the angel of my deliverance, come to lead me to Jesus?

• *Do I trustfully abandon all my past to*
His mercy and my future to His love?

• *Have I finally decided really to enter*
into the life of union with Jesus?

• *What fruit have I gathered from these meditations?*
Am I more truly united to my Savior?

Do I know Him more? Do I love Him better —
with real affection that is put into practice?
As a proof of this, what resolutions
am I now going to make and keep?

∽

Resolution

∽

Spiritual Bouquet
"O my Love, may Thy farewell to
me be sweet in death, and may my
'rest in peace' be full of delights."

St. Gertrude

∞

Sophia Institute Press®

Sophia Institute™ is a nonprofit institution that seeks to restore man's knowledge of eternal truth, including man's knowledge of his own nature, his relation to other persons, and his relation to God.

Sophia Institute Press® serves this end in numerous ways: it publishes translations of foreign works to make them accessible for the first time to English-speaking readers; it brings out-of-print books back into print; and it publishes important new books that fulfill the ideals of Sophia Institute™. These books afford readers a rich source of the enduring wisdom of mankind.

Sophia Institute Press® makes these high-quality books available to the general public by using advanced technology and by soliciting donations to subsidize its general publishing costs. Your generosity can help Sophia Institute Press® to provide the public with editions of works containing the enduring wisdom of the ages. Please send your tax-deductible contribution to the address below. We also welcome your questions, comments, and suggestions.

For your free catalog, call:
Toll-free: 1-800-888-9344

or write:
Sophia Institute Press®
Box 5284, Manchester, NH 03108

or visit our website:
www.sophiainstitute.com

Sophia Institute™ is a tax-exempt institution
as defined by the Internal Revenue Code,
Section 501(c)(3). Tax I.D. 22-2548708.